YOUR GIFT OF ADMINISTRATION

How to Discover and Use It

YOUR GIFT OF ADMINISTRATION

How to Discover and Use It

TED W. ENGSTROM

Thomas Nelson Publishers
Nashville • Camden • New York

To
faithful and loyal
colleagues
in World Vision
who have shared
the burden of effective administration
with me

C O N T E N T S

The "visionary," a charismatic leader full of zeal and passion, can usually launch an organization of people into initial action. But the honeymoon will not last forever. That's why it takes a leader with administrative skill and judgment to sustain the momentum that vision creates. And because some well-intentioned men and women in the past have ignored this simple reality, more than one worthy organization begun in a blaze of enthusiasm has disintegrated in painful and humiliating failure.

This is why *Your Gift of Administration* is such an important addition to the reading list of any of us who have been granted the privilege of leading people. For in writing it, Ted Engstrom has made it possible for would-be leaders to look beyond the birthing stage of organizational visions. He calls us to appreciate the ongoing process of what it means to create an environment where tasks can be accomplished and where people are provided with an opportunity to achieve the fullness of their God-given potential.

After many years of effective organizational leadership, my friend Ted Engstrom has mingled his experience, his biblical insight, and his personal conviction to give us this new perspective on the exercise of administration. And speaking with unrestrained self-centeredness, I couldn't be more thankful.

As a pastor for more than twenty years, I have learned the hard way that directing the efforts of people and trying to bring out the best that individuals can offer takes more than smooth words and slick ideas. I say that I learned the hard way, because the strategic task of administration was not adequately identified or taught when I was training for ministry.

Because there has been some reluctance to affirm the fact that administration and organizational leadership is a revealed and bestowed gift of the Holy Spirit of God, many well-meaning people have shunned an in-depth study of the subject. "Too business-oriented," they say. Or, "The whole subject smacks of manipulation." And, sadly, some have proposed that administrative work lacks true spirituality—in spite of the fact that Scripture contains many thrilling case studies of management and administration. Moses, Joshua, Ezra, and Nehemiah were administrative giants. And don't forget Joseph of Egypt. When it comes to administrative leadership, these men rank among history's very best.

Now, thanks to Ted Engstrom, we have a chance to examine the nature of the significant role of the administrator in Christian context. He provides guidelines for spotting the signs that indicate a gift of this sort may be within us or in one of our colleagues. And he provides a biblical study of administration which is needed by all of us who have been given the gift of leading people.

Dr. Gordon MacDonald
Pastor, Grace Chapel
Lexington, Massachusetts

The writing of a book resembles in some ways the work of administration. It involves defining the principal message or goal, planning for the project, and finding those who can best assist in the creative process.

In the writing of this book I have had the inestimable help of my good friend Bob Owen. During the planning and writing we met on a number of occasions, discussing many items and incidents at length. He offers the following observations.

My close association with Dr. Ted Engstrom over several years as an editor and a friend has given me some valued inside awareness of the way he conducts his office, the nerve center of his vast responsibilities. There is no getting around it: "Dr. Ted" runs a tight ship.

But that one fact in no way detracts from another: Ted Engstrom is beloved and admired as a man of mercy, vision, resourcefulness, and careful control of his own time and energies. And he conducts his own personal life according to the principles portrayed in his numerous books.

More than any other trait, though, Ted is admired and respected as a leader of principle. He is a man of his word.

I count it an honor to have shared his thoughts and dreams during the months of shaping and writing the essence of his life gift in the finished form which you now hold in your hands.

And so of my friend "Dr. Ted" I say, as it was said of David, when God brought him from tending sheep to caring for Israel, "So he shepherded them according to the integrity of his heart, And guided them by the skillfulness of his hands" (Ps. 78:72).

Bob Owen

The Gift of Administration:
Two Key Factors

One of the great frustrations of life comes in trying to work enthusiastically for a person with official rank in an organization but who has little ability to get the job done.

In the business world such a person is described as "incompetent." In fact, an entire book has been written which describes the problem most entertainingly—*The Peter Principle*. The author pinpoints the problem as that of promoting a person within a corporation to one step above his *level of competence*. A person is given the authority to lead, but he does not have the ability.

As a Christian, I have seen something similar happen in churches. A warm, godly man is ordained pastor. Despite his own devoted personal life, within six months it becomes evident that he is simply inept at shepherding his flock. He is not strong as a leader nor can he administrate the daily affairs of the congregation.

It happens in sports—especially on the college and professional level. A defensive coordinator, say, who has been a friend of all and has produced league-leading pass defense units for years, is named head football coach. People still love him personally, but he cannot effectively mold the coaching staff around him. The players become disgruntled, team mo-

13

mentum is lost, and after three losing seasons he is replaced by someone from outside the organization.

If you think these administrative mismatches are troublesome to the people in the organization, try stepping into the shoes of the leader! Whether this executive or pastor or head coach actually identifies the problem or not, life is incredibly —almost unbearably—full of internal suffering, frustration, and anger.

The Situation in Reverse

Then, just the opposite situation occurs. Let me use just one instance to illustrate what I mean.

Let's take a close look at a political precinct organization. The people are united in purpose; they like each other and have been successful over the years in getting party candidates in office. What's their secret?

A fifty-six-year-old widowed grandmother. She's hardworking, articulate, and dogged in her determination. How long has she been in charge of the precinct structure? She never has. Well, wait—that is not quite accurate. She's never been an officer. "Too busy, too much domestic responsibility now that Jack is gone," she has told the nominating committee for each of the last several years.

But she makes the precinct organization *go*. And there's even a phrase to describe her. "She's our *charismatic* leader," her colleagues insist. But she's never held an office in her twenty years of service.

A Fact of Life

What we have described above is a universal truth about leadership. I would surmise it has been present from the beginning of civilization and will continue on to the end. There are

two components of leadership, two gifts of administration—
official and *charismatic*.

We have on one hand the authority, the office, the place in
the hierarchy from which the job is carried out. There are different words to describe how you get there. In business, you
are *promoted* or *appointed*. In politics you are *elected* or perhaps *succeed* the mayor due to death or resignation. This is all
visible, definable, objective. It is accompanied by ceremony,
dignity, pomp—banquets, speeches, sometimes even parades.
Someone has taken office. Official authority—who is in
charge—is now settled.

On the other hand we have an invisible, emotional, inspirational sort of administrative dynamic at work. Wearing a dark
pin-striped suit, a letter jacket, or an alb and stole is not of
first importance for this kind of leader. Instead of words like
"appointed" or "elected," you hear things like, "I don't know
what it is—she's just *got* it." Or, "Old Charlie has kept this
place running for thirty years." Or, "Even though he's third-
string, he's the inspiration of the whole team." Nothing really
official here, is there? No, this is *charismatic* leadership.

Fusing the Factors

Aha! says the careful reader. The secret is to get these two
administrative factors together—the gifted person in the official role. Precisely! And that is what this book is about.

But I want to deal with more than just the basic problem of
the right person for the right job. I want to talk with words of
encouragement and support to those men and women who,
having leadership roles in terms of *office*, feel they need to
develop their administrative *gifts* to better carry out their
roles. I want to assure you that you *can* strengthen your leadership gifts.

I want to talk to those naturally gifted people who bring out the crowds, who captain their teams because of raw talent, but who are inefficient in office. There is a price to pay for relying primarily upon charisma and attractiveness. Others in leadership under you feel passed by and become competitive. The larger group itself will begin to grumble and murmur—and you will be replaced.

My purpose, then, is twofold: to help official leaders develop and strengthen their administrative gifts; to help gifted leaders become more thorough and effective in their official and administrative responsibilities.

To accomplish this task, I have divided this book into three parts.

Part I   Administration as a Personal Gift
Part II Administration as an Office or Function
Part III Growing in Administrative Effectiveness

Part I of this book, which includes chapters 2 and 3, covers the charismatic side of administration—the personal gifts—named in Romans 12:6-8. These are spiritual gifts given to the Christian leader, "he that ruleth," as the old King James Version describes him. I'm going to use the term "personal gift" to deal with these particular gifts of administration.

These chapters will do several things. First, they will help those of you who possess gifts or abilities to administer without being aware of it. Second, these chapters will clarify the *reason* why you may approach your tasks of service as you do. We will define your "administrative mode." Third, there are many of you who are in middle-management roles—business people, music directors in churches, associate pastors, staff physicians, department managers, journalists, contractors, teachers—who possess the gift of administration. Chapters 2 and 3 are designed to help you better understand your administrative gift and to learn how you can strengthen and develop it now, *before* that next step up.

Part II analyzes administration as a *function*, or *office*. As we will see from Ephesians 4:11 and 1 Corinthians 12:28–29, there are numerous functions, or offices, in the Body of Christ. God the Father is so precise, He has personally seen to it that His people have been given all the offices or authorities necessary to accomplish the task He has set before us. These offices can be found functioning in our churches, social service associations, and organizations that assist the Body of Christ. These offices are also found where Christians serve institutions of education, communications, the professions, and a host of similar arenas.

In this second section I will show there are many "styles" of administration which quite naturally emanate from various personality types. It happens that my own personality reflects a directive, methodical leadership, which is the basis of my own administrative style. However, it does not always matter what your own personal gift may be, because *administration as an office, or function, can also be a developed skill.* In chapters 4 through 6 I clarify the official role and spell out ways to more effectively carry it out.

Part III explains how to put the *charismatic* and *official* sides of administration together. It is here we will blend gift and office, to make you more effective in administration for God's glory and for your satisfaction.

In these pages I will show you how to develop your administrative skills to become a more successful administrator *as defined by both personal and organizational standards.* And we will consider the *resources* available to attain to that standard.

PART I

ADMINISTRATION
AS A PERSONAL GIFT

The Personal Gift
of Administration

That there is a valid distinction between *gift* and *office* in the sphere of leadership is nowhere as apparent as in the pages of Holy Scripture.

Perhaps the New Testament passage that most readily comes to mind to illustrate the distinction is in Acts 6, when the apostles in Jerusalem needed special assistants to better care for the church. These assistants were selected to become functionaries to serve Christ's church, and that day their role became an *office* which has lasted in the church for nearly two-thousand years—the diaconate.

But who was selected to fill the role? Just any available saint with a heart for serving God and some free time? Not exactly, though a warm heart and accessible time would certainly figure in. What the apostles wanted and the people agreed to was men who were *gifted*, spiritually equipped to handle the task at hand. Note the biblical text:

> Then the twelve summoned the multitude of the disciples and said, "It is not desirable that we should leave the word of God and serve tables. Therefore, brethren, seek out from among you seven men of good reputation, full of the Holy Spirit and wisdom, whom we may appoint over this business; but we will give ourselves continually to prayer and to the ministry of the word."

21

And the saying pleased the whole multitude. And they chose Stephen, a man full of faith and the Holy Spirit, and Philip, Prochorus, Nicanor, Timon, Parmenas, and Nicolas, a proselyte from Antioch, whom they set before the apostles; and when they had prayed, they laid hands on them (Acts 6:2–6).

An ideal combination, is it not? Gifted men to take official duty.

Was the work these seven deacons were chosen to do something new? No. In fact, this is what made their work an office. Prior to this account in Acts 6, who had done this work? The men who laid hands on them to inaugurate their new roles— the apostles. And where did the apostles receive the authority to pass this work of care and function on to these who became deacons? From our Lord Jesus Christ, who called and gifted them by the Holy Spirit under the oversight of His Heavenly Father.

And did this new arrangement prove productive? Without question. When these gifted men took office and began to function and to serve, "the word of God spread, and the number of the disciples multiplied greatly in Jerusalem, and a great many of the priests were obedient to the faith" (Acts 6:7).

We see a similar unfolding of events come to a head in Acts 13. Here, Paul and Barnabas were set into office.

As they ministered to the Lord and fasted, the Holy Spirit said, "Now separate to Me Barnabas and Saul for the work to which I have called them." Then, having fasted and prayed, and laid hands on them, they sent them away (Acts 13:2–3).

At first glance, one would assume they began that day to minister together. But that is not the case. For they had already worked together in Antioch for an entire year (see Acts 11:25–26). Later this discipling duo took care of the relief work in Judea, (see v. 29) finally returning to Antioch from Jerusalem at the close of Acts 12. It was only after this proven ministry had occurred that Paul and Barnabas were officially set apart in Antioch to begin the first of what have come to be called the three missionary journeys of the apostle Paul. Gifted men again took office.

This gift-office distinction is seen even more often in the Old Testament. When God called Moses to lead the nation of Israel out of Egypt, He also chose an able assistant in Aaron. Look at the dramatic use of both gift and office as God establishes an authoritative relationship between these two kinsmen in Exodus 4:15–16. God said:

> Now you [Moses] shall speak to him [Aaron] and put the words in his mouth. And I will be with your mouth and with his mouth, and I will teach you what you shall do [gift]. So he shall be your spokesman to the people. And he himself shall be as a mouth for you, and you shall be to him as God [office].

In Numbers 11 when Moses needed help in overseeing this same nation in the wilderness, God instructed Moses to select seventy elders to assist him. And look at the Lord's promise in verse 17 for the anointing of these men to serve in the official new capacity. "I will take of the Spirit that is upon you and will put the same upon them [gift]; and they shall bear the burden of the people with you, that you may not bear it yourself alone [office]."

Add to these the appointment of such Old Testament administrators as Joshua, Gideon, David, and Samuel; and the tradition of leadership as both charismatic and official becomes even clearer. Thus it is against this background that the whole matter of spiritual gifts takes on an even richer significance.

In Romans the way gifts relate to office becomes especially clear. Paul writes, "and all members have not the same *office*:

So we, being many, are one body in Christ, and every one members one of another. Having then *gifts* differing according to the grace that is given to us, [let us use them]" (12:4–6 KJV, italics added).

The word "gifts" here derives from the Greek word *chara*, meaning "joy" or "gladness." Therefore it may be said that a person's *charisma* is a special gift given him by God and that the intrinsic nature of the gift is joy. It follows, then, that when a person discovers his or her gift, the awareness of that gift— and the use of it—bring enthusiastic joy and gladness.

These gifts of grace are special to each recipient. And since they are given, we don't have to strive to possess them. They come from the Holy Spirit who lives within us.

My understanding of Saint Paul in Romans 12:4–6 is that every person possesses at least one of these *charismata*, and that God's gifts work in connection with each Christian's personality—also given to him by God. I call these charismata "personal gifts." There are seven such personal gifts listed in this twelfth chapter of Romans, namely: prophecy, ministry, teaching, exhorting, giving, ruling, and mercy.

For the purposes outlined in this book, I will be addressing primarily the sixth one, described by translators as "he that ruleth" (KJV) or "he who leads." It is this personal gift which designates administrative ability. It derives from the Greek word *proistēmi* and is variously translated "rules," "takes the lead," "to be over," "to superintend," "preside over." I call this particular charisma "the gift of administration."

As Christian believers we have available to us, through the incarnate Christ and the indwelling Holy Spirit, the personal attributes of God the Father. These characteristics are listed in Galatians 5:22–23 and are called "the fruit of the Spirit." This is not something God gives us all at once in full-blown finished form. Instead, when we are joined to Christ, He gives us the seed of each part of this cluster to be nourished and to grow. In chapters 6 through 13, I will discuss what I have learned personally about developing the gift of administration in light of the fruit of the spirit for more effective administration.

The Gift of Administration

Exactly what is this gift? Is this gift differentiated from other personal gifts? Must one possess the gift of administration in order to be able to function as an administrator?

I would not be completely honest if I did not tell you at the outset that I—and those who know me best—believe my primary spiritual gift is that of administration. I am literally motivated to administer, and I have spent the bulk of my adult life serving in leadership roles.

As a young man I went to work for the Zondervan Publishing House as an editor, because I had a great desire to be a writer and publisher. Although I went to Zondervan believing that my duties would basically consist of writing, I soon found myself serving in an administrative position as production and advertising manager, as well as editor. As I developed schedules, worked with printers, produced books (and got them out on time), I began to be aware of God's call on my life to the *function* of administration.

A dozen years later Dr. Bob Cook and Dr. Torrey Johnson were moved by the Spirit of God to invite me to come to Youth for Christ International as an administrator. I served as that organization's president for a number of years, then the leaders of World Vision (moved—I believe—by the Spirit of God) called me to serve in that organization at first as its executive vice-president. And here I have happily remained for the past twenty years.

As I stated earlier, the word used in the Greek text to designate the gift of administration is *proistēmi*. In its usage in Romans 12:8 the word is not referring to an administrative post or office, but to an *administrative gift or motivation*. Or, stated another way, the one who has this gift has an administrative approach to situations.

As one endowed with the personal gift of administration, I approach practically every situation I face in the "administrative mode." This fact is evident to my wife, to my children, and to my colleagues. Dorothy, my wife, would be the first to testify that I become very restless on the inside if my calendar is not in order. I seek to have my schedule and plans organized well in advance if I am to be at ease. I do not operate well in disorder. I am built to know where things stand, to whom I report, for whom I am responsible, and where we are going down the line.

This is not to say there will be no changes in my plans, for these always occur; but I must have a continuing sense of direction for my days—time allocated and scheduled for worshiping God, for being with Dorothy, for handling work loads, for attempting creative activities. And Dorothy knows from my calendar how our schedules fit and mesh together. This, for me, is operating in an "administrative mode" in a personal sense. And living this way is indescribably satisfying.

This does not mean, by the way, that everyone should aim for the same degree of order, long-range planning, and hierarchical sensitivity that I do. To misquote the apostle Paul, "All are not administrators, are they?"

But it is precisely at this point that we learn from each other and we complement one another in the Body of Christ. For example, I have a constant need to spend time around what I call the "prophetic types," those who think, preach, and serve radically and creatively. Such people stretch me and help me see my schedule as a guideline instead of a prison. Similarly, prophetic people need people like me. Administrative types help keep prophetic types on track, ordered, scheduled; so their creativity does not become confusion.

There are many people who would give their eye teeth if they never had to lead. Being anonymous and free from endless responsibility is, for them, the next thing to heaven. Others, if they cannot be there in the thick of things—molding, shaping, directing—are of all men most miserable. Is theirs a play for power, a self-aggrandized appetite to rule and lord it over others? Not at all, or at least not for those motivated and energized by the Holy Spirit. For just as an artist wants to paint, a musician wants to play, or an evangelist wants to preach, so one with the gift of administration wants to give active leadership.

I have not always known, by the way, that my personal gift is that of administration. Many of my friends and colleagues have discussed this matter with me. Frequently I have been asked, "But, Ted, how do you *know* that your gift is administration?"

These questioners often seem to listen impatiently to my explanation before interjecting the question they really want to ask, "How can *I* determine whether I possess the personal gift of administration?"

Such a determination is not a simple, one-two-three question-and-answer routine, especially for an older adult. The reason being that so many of us have developed skills and abilities that—unless examined carefully—can conceal or mask the true nature of one's spiritual gifts.

It is important to realize that we do not determine our gifts all by ourselves. Just as a physician would not do exploratory surgery on himself, so we do not determine by ourselves what our gifts and callings are. In the biblical instances cited earlier in this chapter, we see several factors that help us identify our gifts.

First, the Holy Spirit speaks to God's people. This is the "it seemed good to the Holy Spirit and to us" factor. God will speak to you and others who love Christ. If you are the only one you know who believes you are gifted to administer, beware! Just as it strains one's soul to hear an uncalled preacher preach, so it is equally unsatisfying to be led by an uncalled leader.

Second, if you are called and gifted to administer, you will not have to appoint yourself. Both your peers and those in authority over you will take note and at the proper time call you to serve.

Third, we have vivid examples of godly leaders in the Scriptures who were models of administration. Become familiar with them. Mirror your strengths and weaknesses against their performance.

Finally, there should be an amen in your own heart as to your gift of administration. Note I said "should be." There will be exceptions even here. Occasionally some will be drafted to lead who have great difficulty believing they can do it. Moses was such a one. Saint Paul may have been another.

A prominent fourth century bishop, Saint Gregory of Nazianzus, one of the greatest theologians on the Holy Spirit the church has ever known, was most strikingly in this category. He was ordained a pastor against his will. Later, after he steadfastly refused the pleas of his fellow Christians to become their bishop, the people literally brought him before the episcopate for consecration. While he never doubted God, he questioned his own gifts. Nevertheless, he had a brilliant career defending orthodox Christianity against the heretics. But he did insist on taking "early retirement," stepping down in his early fifties to return to seclusion, study, and prayer.

A Variety of Service

Certainly not all who administer do so in the same way.

And not all who lead must specifically possess the gift of administration. Other gifts may also be effective in an administrative post.

George Marhad is one of my colleagues at World Vision. George is serving in an administrative function as my assistant because he has well-developed leadership skills. While George's primary personal gift may appear at first to be that of administration, such is not the case. I have watched George operate; and while extremely effective, he approaches everything he does in a more nonadministrative manner than do I. The traits which the Scriptures associate with the gift of administration simply are not there. George approaches his daily tasks from the base of his personal gift of exhorting. By contrast, I insist on thorough planning and step-by-step organization of any project before I will proceed. Then, when the project is securely underway, I proceed straight ahead regardless of obstacles that would hinder the attainment of set goals.

George does things differently. He has learned to plan well, and usually does so. But he has a very strong aversion to pushing ahead to achieve the intended deadlines and goals if doing so will impinge upon the pride or feelings of his coworkers. Whereas I will often move ahead and soothe feelings as I go, George will tend to halt the project until the people he is working with are encouraged to continue.

I think you can see what I am illustrating in this thumbnail sketch of the two of us. I love and respect George. He loves and respects me. We have worked together harmoniously for years. We are both effective administrators. But we approach many things differently. And any administrator who approaches the task with a primary personal gift other than administration (say prophecy, ministry, serving, or teaching) will administer the responsibilities differently from one whose personal gift is administration.

Traits of a Gifted Administrator

Having discussed the sense of teamwork in the church in determining the gifts of the Spirit, let us look at some commonly recognized traits of those possessing the gift of administration. Dr. Hugh Ross, associate minister of evangelism for the Sierra Madre Congregational Church in Sierra Madre, California, leads numerous groups in understanding the gift of administration. He has compiled a representative list of attributes and the various ways of motivating a person who possesses this gift. Often a list of this nature appears as an appendix in a book. But I have found it so useful, I am using it here in the text, with his permission, because I believe that you will find it valuable as well.

Character Qualities and Personality Traits of Those Possessing the Personal Gift of Administration

1. Possesses an ability to integrate several ministries, people tasks, and/or projects towards the fulfillment of a long-range goal.
2. Is sensitive to future needs, particularly to future needs that are not being planned for by others.
3. Has an ability to visualize overall needs and to clarify long-range goals.
4. Has an ability to assist an individual Christian by designing and setting up a ministry that offers that Christian the greatest personal satisfaction because it makes the fullest use of the individual's talents, resources, and gifts.
5. Has an ability to put together individual Christians to form efficient, well-organized teams—teams on which the members work well together, divide their labor efficiently, and enjoy each other's company.

30

6. Has an ability to discuss the talents, resources, and spiritual gifts of individual Christians.

7. Has an ability to discern and unify available resources toward the fulfillment of a goal.

8. Tends to avoid involvement in anything for which he has no organizational responsibility. Furthermore, his tendency is to remain on the sidelines until the leaders in charge turn responsibility over to him.

9. Tends to assume responsibility if no structured leadership exists.

10. Desires to see that his time and the time of others is used efficiently.

11. Tends to insist on thorough planning and organization before embarking on a new task or new ministry. Tends to avoid the develop-as-you-go type of ministries or projects. He wants things done right from the beginning.

12. Demonstrates a willingness to wait on a project or ministry until it is properly set up. Once a project is set up, however, he will push for maximum speed in accomplishing its goals.

13. Is strongly motivated to organize anything for which he is responsible.

14. Has an ability to make use of the resources available at the present time, not waiting for future resources to develop.

15. Is motivated to delegate, if at all possible.

16. Has an ability to know what can or cannot be delegated.

17. Is sensitive to recognize and to acknowledge other people's hidden achievements that have helped in reaching a goal.

18. Tends to put high priority on loyalty in selecting people for a team.

19. Tends to be neat and orderly in everything: home, appearance, job, other activities (even recreation), and projects.

20. Is reluctant to pay for organizational services, preferring to perform these himself. He prefers to make proposals rather than ask for bids. He wants to be his own contractor.

21. Tends to assign tasks or solve problems with his eyes on the future impact of his decisions and actions.

22. Is able and willing to endure reaction from others in order to accomplish an ultimate goal in a minimum amount of time. He recognizes that others are not as sensitive as he may be to the overall picture or to the importance of the goal.

23. Is strongly motivated to help others become more efficient in carrying out tasks.

24. Recognizes the importance of maintaining good records and of writing clear instructions. He sees that with these aids a task can be easily repeated in the future or in some different context.

25. Places a high premium on reliability and responsibility. He tends to react to people who do not follow through and help with the cleanup or with the behind-the-scenes work.

26. Tends to avoid the limelight; however, he definitely enjoys the role of a strategic commander working behind the scenes, pushing pawns on the game board of life.

27. Tends to remain firm and steadfast, regardless of opposition, once he has determined that a particular goal is in God's will.

28. Believes strongly in the importance of keeping commitments even in adverse or difficult circumstances.

29. Appreciates initiative. He values people who can fore-see problems and take action to prevent or correct them without having to get detailed instructions.

30. Demonstrates an ability to finalize difficult decisions, though he is very careful and deliberate to first examine all of the pertinent facts.

31. May appear to be a perfectionist because he insists on detailed planning and preparation.

32. May tend to overlook spiritual weaknesses and faults of key persons on the teams that he designs because he focuses almost solely on the personal talents, training, and spiritual gifts that will be useful for achieving a particular goal.

33. If problems exist in his organization, tends to handle them by readjusting the responsibilities and positions of individuals on the team in order to achieve more compatible working relationships (as opposed to first solving individuals' personal problems).

34. May tend to view people impersonally as resources available for helping him achieve goals. People working for him or with him may feel that they are being used.

35. May appear callous to those who misinterpret his willingness to endure reaction.

36. May appear insensitive to the weariness, schedules, and priorities of people on his team because of his strong desire to complete a given task as quickly as possible.

37. May appear lazy or skilled in avoiding work because of his ability and willingness to delegate responsibility.

38. May cause others on his team to feel that they are being misused if he fails to explain thoroughly enough the reasons why their tasks must be done within a certain timespan.

39. Is strongly motivated to look for and move on to a new

challenge whenever a project comes to completion. If this motivation is highly exercised, he may get the reputation of being an empire builder.

40. Receives great fulfillment in seeing all the pieces of a project fitting together and in seeing others enjoying the finished product.

As you think back through this listing of forty traits of a gifted administrator, do you find they correlate generally with your own abilities and desires? Did you note the traits that promote negative feelings in others? If you have chafed under the leadership of another, does the list motivate you toward more tolerance and understanding?

If you are currently involved in active administration, you no doubt can see areas in which you need to concentrate on improving as you continue to serve. If you aspire to lead, take heart by being patient with God to establish you in His right time.

From my personal viewpoint, as one who is constantly seeking to learn to understand his personal gift, I can say the only greater joy than knowing and understanding what your gift is, is to find yourself functioning in the Body of Christ in an office or role that fits, because it is the one to which God has called you.

An Administrative Approach

I am continually amazed at the intricacies of our bodies. Each organ is miraculous in itself. The eye, prototype for the camera, is astounding in its construction, durability, and capabilities. The brain, with its miles of nerves and neurotransmitters, is far more complex and efficient than today's super computers. And think of the heart, which pumps day and night, without a rest, for three-score and ten years and beyond. Think of the kidneys, the lungs, the digestive tract.

All of our organs are designed by God, the Master Architect and Builder. But perhaps the most exciting fact concerning these physical bodies is their synergism, their interrelation and cooperative action with all the other organs. For when our physical "machine" is operating properly, there is no conflict or competition between any of them. They all operate smoothly as a single unit, a whole.

God's plan was the same for His Body, the church, as it was for our physical bodies—the same kind of synergistic balance, the same smooth blending together of thoughts with actions, the same hand-eye coordination. He planned that there be no schisms in His Body, just as He planned that there be no malfunctioning in our physical bodies.

He planned His Body every bit as precisely as He planned ours. Therefore, even as He equips each individual Christian with a personal gift, He also provides each individual with a place to function within the Body with that gift.

These "places" are called offices, or functions. In order to clarify exactly how we each best fit within God's Body framework, we are going to take a look at several of these offices. But I don't want us to do this in a general way. We are going to look at a few of these offices specifically *from the viewpoint of one with the personal gift of administration* and see how he or she might approach this variety of offices.

If you are a Christian in business, labor, or a profession, you need to know that these next few pages apply primarily to people who are involved in direct Christian service in the church. I will present material that pertains more generally to us all midway through this chapter under the topic Potential Misunderstandings.

Pastor

How would a person with the personal gift of administration function as a pastor? What sort of church organization would he set up? Where would his primary emphases lie?

Such a pastor would probably major in providing a well-organized, smooth-running organization, with every phase and department carried out and functioning with decency and in order.

His administrative approach would be evident in everything he does, from leading his official board meetings to the precise, orderly way he designs and conducts the worship service. The grounds would be well cared for, the property and equipment in good order.

This approach could be self-limiting. If this highly organized pastor served either a small congregation with neither the finances nor personnel to assist in some of the responsibilities of running such an orderly organization, the pastor with a personal gift of administration would: (1) become very frustrated if things did not get done properly and do them himself, expending inordinate amounts of time and energy; (2) find some way to delegate some of the tasks and thus get it all done; or (3) be unable to handle the dissonance over an extended length of time, so he would resign and go elsewhere.

Missionary

In our modern-day church, the man who most closely fits the biblical description of an apostle—one "sent out by the Holy Spirit" (Acts 13:4)—is the missionary. Let us look at this person who is serving in the office of a sent one, the missionary, whose personal gift is that of administration.

What sort of an organization would this person set up and administer? Where would his primary attention be focused? How good an apostle would he be?

What sort of an organization . . . ? Actually, this person would first of all determine the breadth and scope of the work to be done, then design an efficient plan to encompass it all in the most effective manner.

For instance, if the missionary organization had planned to set up and run an effective Bible training school, reach out into new areas with the gospel message, and produce a New Testament in the native language, then this missionary would probably develop a schedule, delegate workers, teachers, and other personnel to get all of these projects accomplished in the shortest time possible.

In time the school would be built, the new areas ministered to, the language would be mastered, and the New Testament translated and published. And all of it would be smoothly run and administered by this missionary who had the personal gift of administration.

Those Who Help

The third function we will investigate is that of helps. This little-understood office is one vitally needed by the body as a whole. It is my personal opinion that the church already has plenty of generals, but too few who are willing to be privates.

Having personally visited literally hundreds of churches and talked to pastors of all theological persuasions, I know the general cry is, "We need more people who are willing to help . . . to help do anything and everything that needs to be done." Such are those who serve in the function of helps.

Now for the question: What would they do, and how would they do it, if they are persons whose personal gift is that of administration?

There was such a man in a nearby large church. He was a retired businessman who began to make a list of things around the church property that needed to be done. He found some willing young people in the church and delegated duties to them. The man's hobby happened to be gardening. He saw that the lawns were not being properly fed, the shrubs not trimmed, and that a number of the lawn sprinklers were in need of repair.

So, without any fanfare, he enlisted the aid of a few others, purchased the necessary materials, and got everything repaired. This man's personal gift of administration was of tremendous value as he served in the office of helps.

Teacher

Another office I want to mention is that of teacher. People with the personal gift of administration serving in the office of a teacher would undoubtedly produce logical, well-planned, well-organized teaching materials and studies. They would have their sessions planned for weeks or months in advance.

Each class would know exactly what was coming, exactly what would be expected of them. And how would they know? They would receive carefully prepared assignments and regular updates. Teachers with the personal gift of administration are a special boon to any learner.

Administrator

The last office I will mention in this context is that of administration. This is the area with which I am most familiar. I recognize my personal gift as that of administration and the office to which I have been called is that of an administrator. I can say, "I am an administrator whose personal gift is that of administration."

And how do I administrate? Briefly, I seek to advocate, design, and set up a smoothly running, well-functioning organization. I am a stickler for plans, programs, goals, and achievements. Goals and plans excite me, so I plan. Achievements excite me, so I seek to achieve.

But I don't do it alone. I delegate. I enlist the aid of others. We sit down together and look at the overall projects to be accomplished, then we plan how best to see them through to completion. That, in a nutshell, is the way I work. It is probably the way any other administrator works whose personal gift is administration.

Potential Misunderstandings

How does an administrator—in the Christian or secular sphere—anticipate possible misunderstandings and deal with them effectively when trouble appears in the wings? Let me mention four areas where misunderstanding often occurs.

1. *One's ability to delegate responsibility may be interpreted as work-avoidance.* As an administrator, you may have faced

this charge. I have on numerous occasions, as have most active administrators. We have merely learned that we can accomplish more for the big picture by standing back, analyzing the scope of the total program, then finding willing hands to do it all. My philosophy is that since I have only two hands, one mind, and so many hours in which to use them, and I have the ability to analyze a situation, project goals and timetables, *and* organize people around a common cause, I can accomplish more by delegation than by trying to do it all myself.

2. *By considering people as resources, the administrator may be charged with valuing projects as more important than the people themselves.* And in a way, this charge is true, though in principle it is not. I deeply value people as individuals. I have a host of good friends among my colleagues at World Vision and throughout the church world. We have mutual respect for one another. However—and this is important for them to understand—when goals are set and deadlines agreed upon, then *barring emergencies, those agreed upon goals will be achieved.* If individuals are incapable of fulfilling their responsibilities, other arrangements will necessarily be made.

When a project is examined, and even before the target date is set, one of the most important considerations is *the people.* I ask myself and the others involved if they believe they are capable of following it through to completion against all obstacles. If the answer is yes, then they are selected. If the answer is no, they will then be given another task in which they can succeed. It's as simple as that. That's how task-oriented administrators work.

3. *The drive to promptly and swiftly execute tasks regardless of obstacles could be considered as insensitivity to the personal priorities or weariness of colleagues.* This charge is related somewhat to the previous one. The key word in this item is "swiftly." On occasion I have been forced to push harder than usual to complete a task, but not as a rule.

Basically, when goals have been set and projects are underway as planned, all of the above considerations have already been computed. It is only when something goes awry, or when certain individuals are unable to contribute their part to the project, that it might become necessary to push a little harder to meet a schedule.

An example of this could occur in our magazine publishing schedule. The printing and mailing dates are set by the year, along with the necessary ancillary systems. If the editor becomes sick and cannot finish the issue one week before our magazine is to be completed, that necessitates a doubling up of other qualified workers in order to get it out on time. If this was not done, either the mailing or the printing dates would be missed and over one million magazines would neither be printed nor mailed, with the resultant loss of considerable income—God's money! So you see, administrators must sometimes make decisions that appear insensitive and callous, when in reality they are not.

4. *One's ability to endure the reactions of others may be interpreted as insouciance.* Since I know that there are quite likely going to be those who won't like what I do or how I do it, I have determined within myself that those negative criticisms will not deter me. Although this may appear callous, in reality it is not, for there are areas of my personality that I recognize as being quite sensitive. But allowing negativism to affect my job is not one of them. I again seek to set goals, calculate possible obstacles or oppositions, make the necessary adjustments—and then "run with the job."

There is a basic similarity in each of these four administrative trouble spots; all of them are reflections of the critical attitudes of others. I must continually remember that I am not responsible for the attitudes that others may adopt concerning me or my work but that I *am* responsible for my own stewardship, my own productivity. If I allow my awareness of how others view me to paralyze me into inactivity, then I will be no better steward than the one in Jesus' parable who buried his talent because, "I was afraid" (Matt. 25:25).

And yet all of these potential trouble spots do represent areas over which I must carefully guard, lest I indeed become insensitive to the rights and needs of others. I am grateful for God's promise that the Holy Spirit will guide me (and all other Christian administrators) "into all truth" (John 16:13) as I abide in Him (see John 15:7). With such assurances, we can have total confidence in His ability to enable us to lead and work sensitively with the ones for whose administration we are responsible.

PART II

ADMINISTRATION AS AN OFFICE OR FUNCTION

CHAPTER 4

Administration Is a
Ministry Gift to the Body

In addition to providing each individual with a personal gift, as listed in Romans 12:6–8, God has also given *ministry gifts* to the Body of Christ as a whole. The apostle Paul first mentions these briefly in 1 Corinthians 12:5 with the statement, "There are differences of administrations" (KJV).

In this passage of Scripture the word "administration" is translated from the Greek word *diakonia*, which is also defined as ministries, functions, or offices. These *offices*, or *functions*, are listed in Ephesians 4:11 and 1 Corinthians 12:28.

Because the purpose of this book is not to delineate each of these offices which God has set within the Body, I will simply move down to the one with which the scope of this book is dealing. "And God has appointed these in the church . . . administrations" (1 Cor. 12:28). The same word is rendered "gifts of administration" in the New International Version.

It must be understood that we are now speaking about something entirely different from one's personal gift—the *charisma* referred to in Romans 12:6–8. That gift is individual, personal, and one that impacts every area in the life of the recipient. As I have written earlier, that personal gift dictates the person's *approach* to everything he is a part of. Every individual has one of those seven personal gifts.

But the *diakonia*, the ministry gifts listed in 1 Corinthians

12:28 and Ephesians 4:11, are gifts that have been given to edify the Body of Christ; and each believing individual is called to function in one of these ten offices. So throughout this book I shall refer to the ministry gift of administration as the function, or office, of administration.

One of the best definitions I have seen of one who fills the *office* of administration describes this person as "a leader with a clear mandate from God, acknowledged as such by the elders, to guide, to coordinate and integrate the affairs and the ministries of the Body of believers, to oversee the ministry of administration within the Body of believers, and to train qualified Christians in the ministry of administration."

Personally, I believe this definition is scripturally accurate, because our biblical examples follow this pattern. An outstanding illustration of this principle is found in Acts 13. While the Body was assembled (v. 1) and worshiping the Lord and fasting, "the Holy Spirit said, 'Now separate to Me Barnabas and Saul for the work *to which I have called them*'"(v. 2, italics added). The prerequisites are clear. These men had been previously called by the Lord. Now—in response to the Holy Spirit's voice—the spiritual leaders recognized that fact, and they themselves set Barnabas and Saul in a particular office to perform a particular function in the Body.

It is important to understand that the call to serve in any one of these offices named in 1 Corinthians 12:28 and Ephesians 4:11 is *not one that comes immediately even to multitalented individuals.* The call comes to qualified believers who have demonstrated a sufficient level of spiritual growth and maturity, so that they are ready to lead and equip others in that particular ministry office.

This is a biblical principle. The apostle Paul, when writing to Timothy, pointedly instructed him to select only men for administering to the church who were mature in the Word and spiritually stable in the administering of *all their own personal affairs.*

In other words, Paul instructed Timothy not to select someone for leadership in spiritual matters who was not a wise ruler of his own household. Paul knew that if a man cannot rule and administer his own personal matters in a manner pleasing to God, then he should not be set in a position of authority over his spiritual brothers and sisters. In context (using the same Greek word which he used in addressing Timothy) Paul instructed Titus to "be careful to *maintain* good works" in his work for the Lord (Titus 3:8).

The same basic principle that Paul outlined to Timothy and Titus was the one by which the apostles operated during those first years of the burgeoning church of Jesus Christ. When administrative problems arose, "the twelve summoned the multitude of the disciples and said, 'It is not desirable that we should leave the word of God and serve tables. Therefore, brethren, seek out from among you seven men of *good reputation* (the *Amplified Version* says here, "seven men of *good and attested character and repute*"), full of the Holy Spirit and wisdom, whom we may appoint over this business' " (Acts 6:23).

The point here is that the church was not instructed to seek out men with personal gifts, but men who were full of the Holy Spirit and spiritual wisdom, men who were *spiritually mature.* These were the ones to whom God entrusted this important administrative service.

Although God has high standards of behavior for each person He calls to edify the Body, it is clear that He is no respecter of persons (see Rom. 12:11). Let us consider a familiar story from the life of the apostle Peter in the Book of Acts.

Peter had been staying at the seacoast home of one designated only as "Simon, a tanner." About noon one day while Peter was praying, God gave him a vision, the meaning of which was not immediately clear. But as this tenth chapter of Acts reports, God makes the interpretation of Peter's vision very clear.

Peter was to go to the home of a Gentile named Cornelius and share the good news of Jesus, the Messiah, with him. This would have to be an act of faithful obedience on Peter's part because, as a Jew, he was forbidden to have any social intercourse with non-Jews (see Acts 10:28). Peter acted upon God's instructions and subsequently entered Cornelius's home. During the ensuing conversation Peter said, "In truth I perceive that God shows no partiality. But in every nation whoever fears Him and works righteousness is accepted by Him" (Acts 10:34–35).

From this and other Scriptures, I believe God is showing us that He accepts equally the person who functions in the office of administration in obedience to His call and the one who functions in the office of evangelism. I believe the same is true for all of these ministry gifts to the Body: apostles, prophets, teachers, miracles, gifts of healing, helps, governments, diversities of tongues. They are each equal; neither is greater nor lesser than another in God's sight.

God's Word makes it clear that those individuals who respond to the call of administration are just as necessary to the complete edifying of His Body as those responding to any of the other nine ministry gifts. As Peter said, "The people God accepts are the people who hear and obey Him." So God's acceptance of you is not determined by your personal gift or by the office or function to which you have been called, but rather by your obedience to that call. This must be so, for we have many members—both in the secular world and the church (see 1 Cor. 12:14–27)—and God declares them all to be important.

It would be strange indeed if God were to designate a finger to be more important than a toe, or an eye to be more important than a lung. It is clear, of course, that in *some instances* a finger is more important than a toe. It is easier to type a letter with your finger than your toe! And when it comes to breathing, it is obvious that the lung is of much greater importance than the eye.

The same with the Body of Christ. For certain designated purposes, one office would be better than another. Picture a group of strong, healthy young men, all of them eager to prepare themselves for service in the kingdom of God. These young men have no need for healing. They need a teacher. The person functioning in the office of teacher would naturally be of much greater use for the situation than one functioning in the office of healing.

By the same token, imagine the frustration faced by a building full of needy, expectant people, awaiting an evangelist to point them to God. But instead of the expected herald come to proclaim the gospel, who should appear but an administrator! The person functioning in the office of evangelist is of much greater use for this situation than the one functioning in the office of administration.

However, Billy Graham's effective organization would soon flounder if it were not for people like George Wilson and others who have been called by God to the office of administration and placed in the Billy Graham Evangelistic Association by the spiritual elders of that organization. For the most effective and efficient day-by-day managing of even Billy Graham's fine organization, a person functioning in the office of administration is of much greater use than a person called to function in the office of evangelist.

Perhaps, as one called to function in the office of administration rather than in what you consider one of the more prominent of the ministry gifts, you may feel yourself relegated to a second-class-citizen position in the kingdom of God. If such is your experience, you need to read—over and over and over again until the words come alive within your spirit—what God has to say about each part of His Body and about giving honor where honor is due—to *all the special ministry gifts* which He has so generously bestowed upon His Body.

As I have done this, it has become very clear in my spirit that each of the functions are of equal importance in the Body. For special situations one or another of the functions might be emphasized or highlighted. But as you view the ministry gifts in totality, you will find that all of the functions listed in 1 Corinthians 12:28 and Ephesians 4:11 are vitally necessary to the smooth operation of God's kingdom. None is more important and none is less important than the others.

Since each member of the Body has been given a charisma, a personal gift, it naturally follows that each administrator will administer differently from another. The reason for this is that every person serving the Body in an administrative role will *not necessarily* possess the *personal* gift of administration.

In the following pages I will be depicting each of the seven personal gifts in situations *in which the possessor of that gift is serving as an administrator.* By so doing I will be able to demonstrate how each of these personal gifts motivates a person to approach and handle the administrative situation differently.

Before doing this, though, I want to repeat that even though each person approaches the administrative situation differently, one personal gift or approach is not better than another. It may be, however, that there are times when God will call a person with a certain personal gift to an office that, to us, may not seem to be appropriate.

When this does happen and the person is clearly walking in the will of God, the results that follow will bring glory to God.

Let us consider these personal gifts in the order in which they appear in Romans 12:6–8. The first one is *prophecy,* which is evidenced by a strong desire to declare truth. Persons thus gifted are strongly motivated to encourage others to repent of their rebellion against God and to strengthen their commitment to God. They have been gifted with special abilities and capacities for identifying, exposing, defining, and hating evil.

A man I will call Ron is a person serving in an administrative office who has *the gift of prophecy*. He spoke at the Anaheim, California, Convention Center recently. He is vice-president of a large, well-known firm. Though the company is not Christian per se, Ron overtly shares the importance of his Christian commitment wherever he is.

"The company considers me to be an effective administrator," he said, "and has demonstrated their confidence in me in numerous ways. During the past ten years I have considered retiring several times. . . . " (Having been with the company for thirty-five years, Ron is eligible for retirement.)

Each time he has made his intentions known, the president and the board have prevailed upon him to remain. "So I have chosen to remain," Ron said, "not because of the increased income and fringe benefits—but because God has clearly directed me to do so."

As vice-president, there are many hundreds of employees who look to him for leadership and jurisdiction. In all of his involvements, including with his staff and in division meetings, Ron unashamedly shares Jesus Christ. The result is a growing percentage of employees within this secular organization who are following his example.

Although God's placing a man whose personal gift is prophecy *instead of administration* in such an important administrative position might seem incongruous to us, such is not the case. Ron, with his strong motivation to declare the truth of God, is more likely to be an aggressive witness in such a situation than an administrator with a different gift.

A former employee of World Vision illustrates *the gift of ministry*. Gene worked faithfully and well in our mailing

51

operation, then left to organize his own business. The practical manner in which Gene has administered his organization has resulted in excellent growth. Today, after being in business for fourteen years, Gene's mailing business ministers to the needs of scores of Christian organizations.

The reason Gene's business has been so successful is, I believe, because he himself demonstrates the following characteristics which relate to the gift of ministry—the enjoyment of practical people and organizations and the tendency to be practical in all areas.

Coupled with yet another characteristic, that of willingly performing any task that needs doing, Gene's statement, "I love my work and the people I work with," totally fits both the man and the expression of the man's personal gift as he administers his business.

The *gift of teaching* is often demonstrated in one who administers. An excellent example of this is the pastor of a large metropolitan church in Los Angeles. The church began just a few years ago when a handful of people purchased the large property of a church that was disbanding.

In a sanctuary that once seated twelve hundred, four-hundred people "rattled around like a handful of peas in a paper bag." The pastor's gift is teaching, as evidenced by his love of words and definitions, his clear presentation of Bible truths, his logical presentation of material which he has diligently and thoroughly made his own by intensive study, and his overt desire to correct misinformation.

Not only has this pastor taught the people the principles of living practical lives as God teaches, but he has taught them how to use that dynamic power to change their personal circumstances.

So successful has this pastor's administration been, that the original membership of four hundred' has grown to an astounding ten thousand, with a greatly enlarged sanctuary.

"My personal gift is teaching," my friend says, "and the people respond to it. As I utilize my personal gift and approach everything I do in that manner, including the direction of the church program, God manifests Himself to us in amazing ways."

The *gift of exhorting* is one given to those who might also find themselves functioning in the Body as administrators. This personal gift is evidenced by those who are the "encouragers," the "edifiers." The Greek word that has been translated "exhort" is *parakaleo*, and it means "to encourage, implore, appeal to, entreat, comfort, cheer up." It also has the connotation of building up, as in the charging of a battery.

I have mentioned George Marhad, my administrative colleague here at World Vision. George exhibits the personal gift of exhorting by the ability to choose words that encourage, by taking adequate time to make people feel good about themselves, by being able to encourage others regardless of personal circumstances. George enjoys one-to-one sharing and counseling opportunities. Another characteristic of this personal gift of exhorting is that he expresses consistent enthusiasm.

The personal *gift of giving* is a boon to the Body of Christ. This gift is characterized by one who enjoys giving to unpublicized needs, who uses his material goods efficiently for the benefit of others, who is alert to discover places to give that have been overlooked by others.

Kathleen is such a woman. She is the administrator of a large travel agency and as such earns a good salary, which she is very generous with. Her giving is largely unnoticed by those around her for a simple reason—she tells nobody the extent of her generosity. She receives great joy from the act of giving itself.

But one of the major advantages of Kathleen's position is that she has the opportunity to give to missionaries, to pastors, and to those who are serving the Lord in various capacities.

And the gift she extends to them is that of travel. Families travel home from faraway lands; parents visit their missionary children; pastors enrich themselves spiritually and the lives of their congregations by visiting Israel and sharing their insights with others.

All this Kathleen delights in. "It's my joy," she says. "I love to give . . . so I give. It's that simple." She is more right than she knows. The charisma of giving—the gracious gift of joy. She has it, she shares it, and the Body is blessed because she has recognized her personal gift and has obeyed the Lord's call to use it while functioning as an administrator.

Last in the list of personal gifts is that of *showing mercy*. A person with this gift has the special ability of being able to identify with those in distress, as well as the capacity to remove hurt and bring comfort. This person reacts to people who seem to be callous, indifferent. He or she weeps easily and tends to be easily hurt.

Such a one is Duane. He reaches out to the hurting, the hungry, the poor, the lonely, the drug addict, the "street people." All of the compassion indicated by his personal gift of mercy has come to focus in the ministry he has founded to those in prison. He travels to prisons frequently, all across the country. He shares Jesus with them, listens to them, corresponds with them.

Duane has a lovely home which he shares with two other men. But he has a spare bedroom which he says is "open to anybody with any kind of a need." That spare bedroom is usually occupied—sometimes for a day or two at a time, sometimes for months at a time.

Duane administrates his prison work well, including volunteers to help with mailings, letter writing, and visits. He is constantly alert, seeking others to whom he can mercifully administer the love of God.

I believe you can see more clearly what I meant when I stated that each of us (administrators or not) possesses a *personal gift* or *charisma*, a joyous grace gift, the use of which produces great joy. Further, each member of the Body of Christ is called to serve as one of the *ministry gifts* to the church.

As one isolates his *personal gift* and begins to function in his *ministry gift*, then the manifestations of God's blessing and power will flow through him to the entire Body of Christ.

CHAPTER 5

Called to Serve

Paradoxically, one who leads or administers the work of others is the servant of those whom he leads. When analyzed, though, this apparent contradiction is not a paradox at all. One cannot lead unless he knows where he is going. Only then can a person say, "Follow me," and proceed to lead the way.

Know Where You're Going

And one cannot lead the way until he has well defined in his own mind *where* he is going, for *what purpose* he is going, and *how* he is going to get there!

To administrate also means you have decided *who* you will follow. To change Bob Dylan's lyrics just a bit, "You've got to follow somebody." Our Lord Jesus Christ, the King of Kings, served God the Father. "I can of Myself do nothing," Jesus said (John 5:30); and even God the Father does not operate independently of the other two members of the Godhead. Though He is the fountainhead of the Holy Trinity, He always functions together with God the Son and God the Holy Spirit. For us human beings, we either follow Christ in His church or the devil and his servants. It is granted to none of us to function alone.

Of necessity, then, one cannot simply appear on the scene at

8:00 a.m. some bright Monday morning and say off the top of the head, "Let's go, men . . . follow me."

The administrator is not the slave owner.

In a very real sense, the administrator is the servant. In order to lead, one must serve. And not until he has learned how to serve and follow others can he become the optimal leader himself. It was so with the Lord Jesus. With Saint Peter. With the apostle Paul. It is true with all who serve. If they lead, they serve in the fullest sense of the word.

And leadership takes time. It also takes commitment. If the job, the project, the church, the organization is to get moving and stay moving toward its stated goals, the individual at the top must always be moving out in front, setting the pace for service as he leads the followers.

The Best Leaders Are Led

One could well say, then, that the driver is also the driven. He is driven to lead, and as he leads he is driven to be adequate in knowledge. He is driven to be ahead of the followers. Then he is driven to stay out in front and continue to say, "Follow me."

It is often much easier just to follow.

The apostle Paul was a leader, an administrator, an organizer. Yet in his introduction to the Book of Romans he speaks of himself in the third person, "From Paul, a *bond servant* of Jesus Christ, the Messiah . . ." (1:1 *Amplified Bible*, italics added). And while he said, "Imitate me" (1 Cor. 11:1), he also confessed in Corinth, "I was with you in weakness, and fear, and in much trembling" (1 Cor. 2:3).

The Greek word translated "servant" is *doulos*, literally a slave or servant. Peter begins his second epistle with the same introduction, "Simon Peter, a servant [*doulos*] . . . of Jesus Christ" (2 Pet. 1:2).

These great men were leaders, administrators, "out-front" men, yet they served. And Jesus, the greatest Leader and Follower of all, speaking of leadership to His followers, said, "Let . . . him who is the chief and leader [become] as one who serves" (Luke 22:26 *Amplified Bible*).

Implicitly, Jesus is saying that leadership in its very essence is serving. It cannot be otherwise. To lead is to serve. And to serve is to become the servant of those one is leading. Leading is not an easy responsibility. Again it is only when I am applying myself to the utmost that I can say before God, as did the apostle Paul, "Follow my example," and then the vital words, "as I follow Christ's!" (1 Cor. 11:1 TLB). In other words, "pattern your life after mine."

But then one looks at how Paul patterned his life. He summed it up in a phrase, "but *one thing* I do . . . I press toward the goal for the prize" (Phil. 4:13–14).

It is when I have done my homework, it is when I have studied to show myself approved, "a worker who does not need to be ashamed" (2 Tim. 2:15); it is then and only then that I am ready to lead, to administer, and to serve.

Do you see how clearly and pragmatically service helps tie together the charismatic and official elements of leadership? If the stance of serving is taken by the leader, problems are kept minimal. But if the leader seeks to lord it over the followers, trouble will always result.

The Inevitability of Inconvenience

Again and again the knowledge has come to me that being an administrative leader involves serving, and serving so very often involves inconvenience. It isn't always convenient to serve people. I have things I want to do. Yet, as the leader, I am responsible to be available at all times to serve those whom I lead.

58

Sometimes I work my way through the Gospels and meditate upon the way Jesus handled interruptions. You might consider doing the same. He was often involved in meeting the need of one person when another broke in and demanded that He also speak to that need. In every case He paused to heal, comfort, or do whatever was needed, and then proceeded with His original objective.

Never did He rebuke someone with, "Can't you see that I'm busy?"

It is so important to recognize that often what we consider to be "interruptions" are really occasions for God to break through our routines and get to us, or to enable us to minister to someone's need we may know nothing about.

For Jesus, serving also involved ministering to people who were not always easy to deal with. In His case, there were even lepers to be ministered to. I wouldn't go so far as to suggest having "untouchables" to deal with at times, but I can say that I have often had to administer or arbitrate a situation that was repugnant to me. The personalities involved were abrasive or abusive, and I would much rather have suggested they go elsewhere to settle their disputes. But I needed to appropriate the grace of God and serve, by listening.

John Drakeford's excellent book, *The Awesome Power of the Listening Ear* (Word Books, 1967), identifies the importance of hearing another person—objectively and without prejudging. I have learned that it is not easy. Giving careful attention to what others are saying, and not seeking to give glib answers or suggestions before the other individual is completely heard, is so important. It is a lesson that I, for one, have had to learn—and relearn repeatedly.

The Role of Reassurance

Serving also involves offering reassurances. An excellent example of this in Jesus' ministry has to do with a man by the name of Jairus, who was one of the rulers of the local synagogue. Jairus approached Jesus in a distraught state. He fell at Jesus' feet and said, " 'My little daughter is dying. Please come and put your hands on her so that she will be healed and live.' So Jesus went with him" (Mark 5:23–24 NIV).

I am certain that Jairus was immediately relieved, because he knew that Jesus went about healing the sick. But Jesus was suddenly stopped on the way by a woman who needed healing herself. (Now His interruption was interrupted!)

You remember the story. This woman had had an issue of blood for many years. She came up behind Jesus in the crowd "and touched his cloak, because she thought, 'If I just touch his clothes, I will be healed.' Immediately her bleeding stopped" (vv. 27–29 NIV).

Jesus stopped and looked around. He asked who had touched Him. A dialogue ensued with His disciples, then with the woman herself. All of this took time. Meanwhile, Jairus must have despairingly wished they would all go away and let Jesus proceed to his home.

It was while Jesus was still ministering to the woman that some men came to Jairus from his house and told him his daughter had just died. But before Jairus could even respond to them, Jesus turned to him and offered those wonderful words of reassurance, "Don't be afraid; just believe" (v. 35 NIV). Subsequently they reached Jairus's home, and Jesus ministered life to the little girl.

I can only believe that Jesus' words of reassurance strengthened and comforted Jairus along that seemingly endless walk to his home. I also believe that, as administrators, our words of comfort and reassurance when our people become frustrated are often the means of enabling them to continue on during difficult times in their lives.

I know how often colleagues of mine have been lead by the

Spirit to say just the right word to me in times of distress or difficult decision-making. They perhaps did not know they were ministering to me in this way, but God used their word of encouragement at just the right time to bring strength to me in difficult circumstances. As administrators, we can trust Him to do that with each of us as we speak that special, warm word of affirmation when we may not be aware of the burden being carried by an employee or peer.

We're Human, Too

As I have sought to minister comfort to others, I have sometimes wondered (as have other administrators), "Doesn't anybody ever realize that I am human, too?" There are times when we all would like for someone to pat us on the back and reassure us. But it's during times such as these that God meets my own needs through one of his other servants who possesses both the sensitivity and the ability to do so.

One such man is my dear friend and colleague Dr. Carlton Booth. He has been around our office for many years as secretary of our board and a personal counsellor. Carlton has been with both me and the organization through the most difficult as well as the blessedly prosperous times. I have never known a man who is so possessed with the ability to minister love, affirmation, and reassurance at just the right time.

I recall when we were going through the deepest of waters in World Vision upon the resignation of our founder/president, Dr. Bob Pierce, and the struggles we faced as an organization simply to survive. Time without number Carlton said to me, "Ted, stay with us; hang in there. God is not through with us. He has His plans for all of us, and for World Vision. Don't give up or give in." His words of perseverance have been so consistently on target and timely, for years I have called him my Barnabas, my "Son of Encouragement"! (Acts 4:36).

Reach Out and Touch Someone

Serving also means that I must sometimes physically acknowledge others. Personally, I am not much given to touching others—either men or women. It's not so much that I'm averse to the physical contact of touching or that intimacy frightens me, it's just that, to put it in the vernacular, "I'm not into touching." Consequently, I don't often go around hugging people or putting my arm around peoples' shoulders. That's just not me.

However, I realize that Jesus ministered to different people in different ways. Some He touched. Others He merely spoke to. His ministry was not stereotyped. His ministering principle was that He was sensitive to the Father's will for people's needs. And He met each person's need *right where that person was.* Recall the woman with the issue of blood, the demon-possessed man—and so many others.

There are times when possibly the physical touch is the only salve that will provide healing. So on those occasions, as the Holy Spirit directs me, I also seek to provide that physical touch. I've seen, as I'm sure you have, how meaningful a warm hand on the arm with an encouraging word can be to the recipient.

Serving isn't something that comes easily to everyone. Some just don't understand or recognize the important role of service, and to these people it is demeaning to serve or to wait on another. Even the ones who appreciate the ministry of service don't always like to serve continually; and when they do serve, they often want to choose whom they serve.

But for the one who is to administer, I believe it is axiomatic that he is called as much to serve as he is called to administrate. I doubt that the two words can be totally dissected from each other, because implicit in each *is* the other. Neither is complete without the other. In fact, one of Webster's definitions of the word "serve" is "to be used, or be useable."

With this in mind, many of us must rethink our concept of serving. I know of men and women to whom serving carries a negative connotation, the idea of "not being as good as" another person. If you are one of these people, you will tend to resent your service to others. This will necessitate your choosing to accept serving as part of administration by an act of will. Then, through a further act of the will, serving with joy.

Learning to Lead

Let me share a few suggestions that have helped me to do just that.

1. *Institute plans into your life that are conducive to serving.* It is easy for an administrator to think of himself as the one who gives the orders and calls the shots, and hold himself aloof from the "troops." Such an attitude might work for a time, but it will soon break down. Authority must always move hand in hand with service, because the "troops" need a leader who leads by example—not from a distance and by directive only.

Personally, I have sought to develop a practice in my schedule at the office which has turned meaningful dividends for the time expended. It's my regular "walk around." I frequently set aside a couple of hours on a regular basis when I leave my desk and simply walk around our offices. We have five separate buildings, so I seek to offer myself by going to where the people are. I step into our departments and individual offices, greet the men and women, ask how they are doing and simply chat a bit with different ones.

If there are evident needs, I ask about these and briefly discuss means and methods to meet the needs. If something comes up that cannot or should not be handled on the spot, I make a note of it and try to find a way to handle it upon returning to my office.

Many times, even weeks later, an expression of appreciation will come back to me from someone whom I have taken special notice of with a word of encouragement or a question about family, work, or whatever. Again, a simple affirming "word in season" can mean so much (Prov. 15:23). And all it takes is a little thoughtfulness!

2. *Begin patterning your serving after Jesus.* After all, He is the ultimate Server. Study His means and methods of serving. Notice His manner of speaking, His compassionate expressions, His availability. I don't, of course, mean for you to begin speaking or praying in King James terminology, but to live as He lived on earth.

3. *Take a periodic self-inventory.* The following exercise will be useful in helping us look at service in a new light. The quiz below may be one that will help you to get a handle on where you are in a "serving frame of reference." If you will complete the six brief items, you will begin to see yourself somewhat more objectively in the matter of serving. Rate yourself on each question with a score from 1 to 10.

Am I secure enough within myself and in my relationship to Christ to be able to serve others in positive ways without threatening my own self-worth?

Am I truly committed to serving those whom I lead, to actualize their potential?

Am I willing to face the new demands and new disciplines that serving will impose on me?

Am I willing to make daily, decisive acts of self-relinquishment, which is the price often required of those who serve?

Am I willing to take the place of a learner in general, and a listener in particular, to establish and strengthen relationships between myself and the people I serve?

Am I willing to accept as God's purpose that the central meaning of my life is serving?

In the light of the score you give yourself, ask yourself, "Do I consider myself to be one committed to serving?" If the score is lower than 40–45, ask, "What is blocking or hindering my desire to serve?"

A final question that might enable you to better evaluate yourself and to improve your score is, "What definite, precise action should I take in order to serve in a more Christ-like manner?" And then act upon the answer!

If I am to follow Jesus—and, if like the apostle Paul, that is my stated aim—then I will become an administrator who cares enough to serve.

PART III

GROWING IN ADMINISTRATIVE
EFFECTIVENESS

Decisions—
Then Delegations

According to a study of *un*successful executives in more than two hundred firms, conducted by the Laboratory of Psychological Studies of the Stevens Institute of Technology, Hoboken, New Jersey, inability to make decisions is one of the principal reasons that administrators fail. In fact, this inability-to-make-decisions syndrome is a much more common reason for administrative failure than lack of specific knowledge or technical know-how.

Most human beings dislike making decisions. Indecision is generally more comfortable. All of us are conscious of the desire to put off deciding—on most things. But few of us are fully aware of the degree to which habitual inability to make decisions interferes with the realization of our full potential and the attainment of our goals in life. Psychiatrists have discovered that every one of us indulges in all kinds of unconscious devices to cover up our indecisiveness.

Procrastination—just not getting around to doing things—is one such device. Others are allowing ourselves to be swayed by circumstances or leaving decisions to someone else. Sometimes people cloud the issues to such a degree that they leave no basis upon which to make a decision.

Why are decisions so painful that we sometimes go to ridiculous lengths just to avoid making them? One reason is that any decision—large or small—involves the risk of being wrong. And being wrong in business could mean losing a job and/or seriously affect the company's future. Another reason is that every decision involves judgment of goals and values—with risks. However, unless an individual has the courage to make choices and take risks, even when the stakes are high, he is not cut out for administrative responsibility.

Some administrators await the views and reports of subordinates so as to have a crutch to lean upon—someone else to blame. For others, the element of personal popularity enters into a decision. The administrative "boss" may not wish to alienate his colleagues or stand aloof from them.

Harry Truman was certainly correct in understanding that "the buck stops here." The administrator must accept the fact that not every decision he makes will be a popular one. Quoting Truman again, "If you can't stand the heat, stay out of the kitchen."

You *will* be wrong a certain percentage of the time. But after all, one of baseball's greatest sluggers, Ted Williams, hit only four out of ten times at bat! But making the difficult decisions is what strong administrators are for. Responsibility for the consequences of far-reaching decisions is, of course, a heavy burden for anyone to bear. Therefore it is not surprising to see administrators, even with many years' experience, displaying a reluctance to come to grips with a problem that calls for a decision. The famous last words in the annals of business are "He could not make up his mind."

Several years back the captain of a supertanker, bound for London, was sailing in the North Sea. It was winter, when storms on that body of water are unpredictable. Both the weather reports and the barometer forecast extremely heavy weather. A veteran of many years at sea, the captain wondered if he should not put into a French port rather than attempt to make London. However, he delayed making his decision, hoping the storm would pass. By the time he realized his mistake, he was in such heavy seas that he no longer had a choice—the decision had been taken from his hands.

Failure to make up his mind resulted in one of the largest oil spills in fuel tanker history and the pollution of hundreds of miles of beaches on both sides of the English Channel. The cost ran into multiplied millions of dollars, both in loss from the spillage and from law suits. The human factor, too, was costly: the captain's license was revoked and he, along with scores of others, needlessly spent weeks in court. All because one administrator couldn't make up his mind.

The means we use to deceive others and ourselves into thinking that it is not yet time to face a major decision are myriad, but in many instances they can be recognized by telltale phrases which spring to the lips when the mind is not yet ready to make a commitment. Here are a few of them:

"I'm going to need a lot more time to think this one over."

"You just can't rush into something like this overnight."

"I don't want to do anything that's going to upset the status quo."

"The time isn't ripe to go ahead."

"We ought to sit on this idea for awhile."

"I'm going to have to study the situation."

"Let's get a little more collective thinking on this."

"I'm going to wait until all the facts are in."

It is a curiously interesting paradox that sometimes these objections are justifiable reasons for not making a decision at the moment. They are sensible stop-look-listen signs to prevent the catastrophes that might result from off-the-cuff, half-baked thinking. But more often than not, they are excuses. And those results can be catastrophic. Sleeping on a problem, for example, allows time for one's subconscious to contribute to a solution.

But when an administrator turns a request of "let's sleep on it" into a Rip-van-Winkle hibernation, then it becomes an escape mechanism.

There is no doubt in my mind that a sense of urgency must be a predominant characteristic of a good administrative personality. Clarence B. Randall, president and chairman of Inland Steel for many years, stressed the need for this in his book, *Freedom's Faith*.

> Some very able and conscientious men never make effective administrators because their approach to difficult problems is judicial in its quality, rather than dynamic. They concentrate so exclusively on the necessity for doing the best thing that they do nothing.
>
> They lack the sense of urgency required in the fast-moving routine of modern administration. Wise as counselors, they perform an important function in cautioning their impetuous associates against pitfalls that otherwise might have been overlooked; but left to themselves, they will never come up affirmatively with a positive program of action.
>
> Actually, in most business situations, a half-dozen possible plans are proposed, any one of which would work reasonably well; and it is far more important to select one and get on with the job, than it is to prolong the debate until the last shred of doubt as to which is the perfect best can be removed.

Over and over again I have found that it is the human factor in decision-making that often afflicts an administrator and prevents him from taking proper action. Many administrators become immobilized by fear of the consequences of doing the wrong thing.

But mistakes are rarely as final and devastating as they seem to be in the middle of the night after execution. After all, learning can take place even through our mistakes. By and large, mistakes—when they are not extreme—are part and parcel of every administrator's career. As in hits, it's the percentage that counts.

Babe Ruth is another example from baseball. He is remembered as the Home Run King, even though his home-run record has been broken in recent years by Henry Aaron. Of even greater interest, though, is the fact that Babe still holds an as-yet-unbroken record for strikeouts. Yet few people remember his failures. Indeed, *it is the percentage that counts.*

You cannot be a decisive administrator—one who is able to make important decisions that affect the lives and destinies of people—unless you are an individual of *personal conviction.* It's a principle I believe in. All other things being equal, if you will develop your convictions, you can become a forward-moving, decision-making administrator.

Many of the administrator's most important decisions are a choice between different sets of values. Which should take priority over others and why? I like the way Professor David Moore of the Graduate School of Business Administration at Michigan State University put it in an address to students in the early 1970s:

> The administrator's loneliest hours are spent in choosing, not between right and wrong, but between two rights. His most creative moments are those in which he successfully integrates values, bringing diverse ideas together into new arrangements.

Granted that decision-making is an all-important administrative function and that choosing the right decision often spells the difference between success and failure, the next question that naturally arises is: Just how does one go about arriving at the best possible decision in a given situation at a given time?

Here is the list which I use in making decisions for myself in matters that are important to me:

1. Identify the problem.
2. Put it down in the clearest language possible.
3. Examine it painstakingly. Get all the facts you can.
4. List the possible choices open to you and what each choice will lead to.
5. Then make your decision on the basis of the facts, scrutinized by the values you believe in.

Let me give you an example. One of the most serious challenges I've ever had in my life was back in 1960 when I was scheduled to lead forty American Christian leaders to a youth congress in Madras, South India. We were to leave the United States on December 27. On Christmas Eve I received word from Washington, D.C., that all of the visas in our passports had been canceled because we were thought to be a political organization. Several thousand delegates would be waiting for us in Madras, and here was the disturbing news that we could not enter the country.

As I prayed that Christmas Eve and asked the Lord to give me some assurance and guidance, my eyes fell on a phrase underlined in my New Testament from 1 John 3:20, "God is greater." I said to the Lord in my prayer, "Lord, here is a very good chance to prove that you are greater than any government or any mountain to be climbed!"

I went to New York to meet with my colleagues the day after Christmas. There, we received our passports from Washington with the visa page canceled out. I indicated that I would refund their travel costs and they could go back home, or they could come along with me as far as Israel to see what would eventuate. All forty said they wanted to move as far as possible toward the goal of getting to the congress in India.

I left a colleague back in Washington to wrestle with the embassy there and to be in constant contact with the Indian leadership in the capital city of New Delhi.

74

Meanwhile, our group went on to the Holy Land, as scheduled, for a few days. On New Year's Eve I received a transatlantic phone call from my colleague in Washington. His opening word was simply, "Hallelujah." I knew then that God had answered our prayers.

The colleague on the phone indicated that we should go to Beirut, Lebanon, the next day, New Year's Day. The Indian Embassy would be opened at 4:00 P.M., and the visas would be restamped into our passports. Two miracles: (1) No embassy in the world is open on New Year's Day—but they did open the Indian Embassy in Beirut! (2) Never is a visa, once canceled, restamped into the same passport. But they did so for forty of us! We arrived on time and enjoyed great blessing in the Madras Congress!

Care and persistence in applying this five-step method to even minor decisions will increase your capacity to apply it to larger ones. Then eventually, when one of your life's biggest decisions is thrust upon you, the time and effort you have learned to take in developing the faculty of making logical, objective decisions will have endued you with the skills and wisdom to make good decisions in the larger, more important matters.

Every decision you ever make will ultimately be the result of weighing two factors: advantages versus disadvantages. Except for the borderline elements that may not be clear gains or losses, this is exactly like making up a balance sheet. Instead of balancing figures, you balance advantages against disadvantages.

It is well to remember, however, that some benefits greatly outweigh corresponding disadvantages, and vice versa. The appropriate "weights" for each entry are not all equal. Be sure to weigh different factors according to their importance if you expect good decisions from the use of this method.

Benjamin Franklin, our wise American patriot, wrote a letter to Joseph Priestley in 1722 in which he had this to say about his personal decision-making procedures:

> My way is to divide half a sheet of paper by a line into two columns, writing at the top of one "Pro" and over the other "Con." Then, during three or four days' consideration, I put down under the different headings, short 'hints' of the different motives, that at different times occur to me, either for or against the measure at hand.
>
> When I have thus got them all together in one view, I endeavor to estimate their respective 'weights'; and where I find two—one on each side that seem equal—I strike them both out. If I find a *Pro* reason that is equal to any two *Con* reasons, I strike out the three. If I judge some two *Con* reasons equal to three *Pro* reasons, I strike out the five. And thus proceeding, I find at length where the balance lies; and if, after a day or two of further consideration, nothing new that is of importance occurs on either side, I come to a determination accordingly.
>
> And, though the weight of reasons cannot be taken with the precision of algebraic quantities, yet, when each is thus considered, separately and comparatively, and the whole lies before me, I think I can judge better and am less liable to make a rash step; and in fact I have found great advantage from this kind of equation, in what may be called *moral* or *prudential algebra*.

My mention of Benjamin Franklin's formula is not to suggest that all administrators must consciously plod through a long, detailed list before arriving at a decision. Undoubtedly most administrators who have actually proven their outstanding capacity to make sound decisions, often at lightning speed, would say, "No, I never do anything like that! I simply get the important facts, estimate the situation, and decide."

Yet I am sure that if we could peer into the unconscious workings of their minds when they are in the throes of decision-making, we would find that many of the steps outlined above are regularly taken in preparing for that critical event when the decision is to be made.

The benefit to you of this "listing" habit will not be in your conscious minute-by-minute decisions, but in the effect it will have in training your subconscious mind to run through a logical process when the decision-making moment is forced upon you.

Practice the art of making decisions. Seek to develop proper timing. Ask God for wisdom—and be courageous. Learning how to think in a pro/con logical sequence is part of the discipline.

The Art of Delegation

The case histories of unsuccessful administrators from the Stevens Institute of Technology study, mentioned earlier in this chapter, were carefully analyzed in an attempt to isolate specific reasons their administrations had resulted in failure. The first on my list is the inability to make decisions. However, the number one reason on the SIT list is the inability to delegate responsibility.

Hard to believe? Perhaps. Yet the ability to delegate wisely, effectively, and successfully is a much more difficult art than one might think. But when properly used, delegation can greatly increase an administrator's effectiveness. The lone leader is limited in strength, ability, and time; but these three factors are multiplied when he shares his responsibility with others.

By properly distributing work, a Christian administrator can find time to do the most essential tasks—guiding, challenging, and fostering growth in his fellow workers. Obviously, then, it is worth every administrator's serious and continuing attention, for even though an administrator may consider himself reasonably proficient in this field, there is always some room for improvement.

There is a classic story about a quiz given to an officers' training class in the Corps of Engineers. One question concerned the writing of the series of commands necessary to raise a heavy, forty-five-foot power pole upright and put it into the hole that had been dug to receive its base. Many of the officer candidates chewed their pencils on that one. But one bright young man wrote his answer without a moment's hesitation. The instructor later read the succinct winning answer. It was, "Corporal, get that pole up!"

Though that may not have been the precise answer sought, the future general had the right idea. He saw that the essence of good administration is not merely to do the job, *but to get it done.*

Most people find delegation easy to define, but hard to practice. As a matter of fact, delegation seems to be a subject for which there is plenty of preaching, but not much practicing. Many administrators kid themselves into thinking they delegate. They pay lip service to delegation. They go through all the motions, but in the end they refuse to part with any significant segment of the workload. Such administrators hold back their organizations, their subordinates, and themselves.

"I know I should delegate more authority," one of my executive friends admitted, "but I just can't seem to get to it." This administrator's problem is really very simple. He doesn't delegate because he doesn't have the time. And the longer he goes without delegating, the less time he will have.

Some administrators say, "My job doesn't permit any real delegation." This is often claimed by those who are in a serious time bind and are making a sincere attempt at self-analysis. Are there jobs where this is really true?

Obviously, a surgeon cannot delegate surgery, a creative researcher must largely conduct the experiments, and a composer must write the scores. However, here we are concerned largely with direction of activities and not with creative artists or craftsmen.

If an administrator feels that the decision-making elements of his job are such that it is necessary for him to do most of the work personally, he may find it illuminating to take another hard look at what portion of his work *can be handled* by others. With respect to your own job, ask youself these five questions:

1. Is there anything someone else can do *better* than you? Are you taking full advantage of the people on your staff who have more direct knowledge, background, and experience in de-tailed phases of the work?

2. Is there anything someone else can do *instead* of you (even if not quite as well)? "I suddenly realized," a colleague said, "that I was running myself ragged because I was neglecting the 'instead of you' principle. Now I limit myself to *talking* over, rather than *taking* over, the job."

3. Is there anything someone can do at *less expense* than you can? Should certain work be handled by the person on the spot instead of necessitating a trip by you? Or by someone whose total salary cost to the company is much less than yours, even though the job might take that person twice as long?

4. Is there anything someone else can do with *better timing* than you? A less than ideal action taken when it is needed may be more valuable than a delayed, but otherwise perfect, han-dling of a situation.

5. Is there anything that will *contribute to training and develop-ing* someone? It may be worthwhile to set up a special program for this purpose alone, mapping out portions of the work for the year ahead in which key people can participate more fully—perhaps rotating them for further flexibility. If possible, plan ahead for eventual complete take-over of certain segments.

Frankly, there have been times when I have passed over certain administrators for promotion because they had never groomed anyone to step into their shoes. It would take months to replace them, and the job I had to fill couldn't wait that long. Andrew Carnegie once said, "The great administrator is the man who knows how to surround himself with men much abler than himself." This may call for some extra effort and expense in the beginning, but let me give one illustration of the effectiveness of it.

Fifteen years ago a young friend of mine in business asked if he could have lunch with me. In our luncheon conversation he indicated that he was very interested in working at World Vision.

At first I told this young man I didn't know of any position open for him at the time. But after considerable discussion, I realized he was the kind of person who could make a valuable contribution to the long-term program of World Vision. I suggested he come and work as my special assistant for a period of time.

Within weeks, he had carved out an important role in our public relations operation. Over the years he found himself with increased responsibilities, which I was grateful to assign to him, including directing one of our major divisions, becoming a field director in the Philippines and, ultimately, our regional director for Asia.

Recognizing his leadership qualities, I later invited him to come back to headquarters and head up our communications division. I had a strong feeling in my heart that he could well serve as my successor one day as the executive director of World Vision. Bill Kliewer assumed that position and performed nobly.

With him I have sought to apply the Paul/Timothy biblical model. Investing in a person like this takes time, energy, and special thought; but the extra effort really pays off, as I am experiencing daily in my relationship with this gentleman who has become our executive vice-president.

Strangely enough, there are administrators who give mental assent to the importance of delegation, but who never or rarely delegate. In leadership development conferences such a person will enter into a discussion of delegation as an administrative skill as intelligently as anyone else and be fully conversant with all of the concepts mentioned earlier in this chapter. And in ninety-nine cases out of a hundred the individual will be of the firm conviction that he does know how to delegate and that *he is doing so* "to the greatest extent possible."

The last phrase is his "out" for all of his time frustrations. He will convince himself that special features of his work preclude delegation, or that he doesn't have and can't get the caliber of staff needed. However, there are enough administrators with comparable responsibilities who are able to free themselves for real administrative work to strongly suggest that the root cause of this problem must be sought on the emotional plane.

Personally, my experience indicates that frequently such inability or unwillingness to delegate stems from an emotional problem, not a rational one. Failure to delegate is probably caused by something that goes on inside an individual, rather than something that is linked with the external variables. If you realize that you are personally unable to delegate, because of something buried deeply inside, you may benefit from examining yourself in the light of these three checkpoints.

1. Are you fearful that some personal weakness might be exposed if you were to delegate? Is there some anxiety because you feel inadequate to handle the magnitude of your job?

You may have been promoted to your present position because of outstanding achievement in a different field or department, and now find yourself forced to deal with many problems with which you are almost totally unfamiliar. Even your subordinates may actually possess greater background in this new area than you do. One fear is that if you delegate to them, they may find out you don't know as much as they.

2. Is there within you a lack of confidence in the ability of others to do the job?

If the answer to this question is yes, you need to ask yourself if this lack of confidence is based on a valid assessment of the situation or whether it reflects an ego-centered fear of letting others try their wings (and maybe fly above you).

Surprisingly, and disappointingly, it is common to find administrators whose egos demand that they surround themselves with lesser lights, because they believe they will then shine more brightly. Thus, they may actually be creating the very condition they complain about—having no one around to whom they can safely delegate. This condition may stem from either an overriding feeling of superiority over the common run of mankind (in which case no degree of ability on the part of subordinates would suffice) or an unbecoming desire for prominence and position. This latter feeling quite naturally leads to the selection of subordinates of somewhat limited abilities or to a restriction of their freedom to act.

3. Are you concerned with who is going to get the credit? The desire to get personal credit for all the significant work of a department reflects the need on the part of the administrator to be constantly reassured as to his own importance. The more or less normal practice of having all important documents go out over the name of the head of a department is understandable and is usually desirable in preventing confusion as to who is responsible for actions taken. But more extreme forms of control manifest themselves in a complete suppression of the identity and individuality of subordinates.

Actually, all three of these situations are devastatingly destructive—to you, to the organization, and to the kingdom of God. Because "God has not given us a spirit of fear, but of power . . . and of a sound mind" (2 Tim. 1:7).

If God has given you the gift of administration and you have been called either in the Body of Christ or in the world to function as an administrator, then you have been given the ability to appropriate the wisdom of God as you work. If fear—for any reason—comes to you, it is not from God. It is from the master deceiver. And Jesus has given us power over him. "Behold!," Jesus said, "I have given you authority and power to trample upon serpents and scorpions, and (physical and mental strength and ability) over all the power that the enemy [possesses], and *nothing shall in any way harm you*" (Luke 10:19, *Amplified Bible*, italics added).

So, take a hard look at yourself. If you are exhibiting fear or lack of confidence or jealousy—to any degree—God is not pleased. And you are dissipating your strength and energies. Determine to appropriate God's remedy, face yourself in the light of His Word, and thrust the fears from you. You can, if you will!

Let me share several tested and proven guidelines to help you delegate more simply and effectively:

Select jobs to be delegated with care and deliberation. There is a difference in delegating assignments and palming off unpleasant tasks. Before turning over a job, I suggest you ask yourself if you are doing it for your personal convenience or to advance your organization and develop your subordinates. *What* you delegate can be just as important as *how* you delegate.

Match the person to the job. Ask yourself these questions to provide assurance that the person you selected is the right one for the job: Is the person well-qualified and capable of understanding the assignment? Does the person really want the job? Will the rest of your staff gracefully accept your choice?

If the job is going to overstrain the mental capacity of the person selected or requires skills the individual does not have, you are setting up a problem situation. Many subordinates accept assignments because they fear the consequences of turning them down.

Motivate job enthusiasm. Which of these approaches do you think will produce better results? (a) "Alex, I want you to take on this job because I'm too busy to handle it myself" or (b) "Alex, I have to turn over Project X to somebody I can trust. The job is of special interest to the president; that's why I've always handled it myself. It requires seasoned judgment; and since you've already done some fine work in this area, I think you're the best person for the job."

Build confidence through training and guidance. You can allay any misgivings from the start. One way is to give the person receiving the assignment all the knowledge and guidance needed to do the job. There are still a minority of administrators who persist in the notion that their hard-earned knowledge is too precious to share and that the more closely they hoard it the more precious it becomes. In practice the reverse is true. The most profitable way to put knowledge to work is by sharing it. And one of the best ways you can share knowledge is by delegation. Then, as the knowledge begins to take hold, you can shore up the person's confidence at regular intervals by expressing how pleased you are with the progress being made and with your choice for the assignment.

Define duties clearly, but not rigidly. A job description that is too broad is likely to leave the person confused about what is expected. A too-rigid definition may restrict the exercise of any initiative. A subordinate's understanding of an assignment is critical. If the role and responsibility are not clearly understood, the assignment cannot be performed acceptably.

Encourage independence and initiative. Theodore Roosevelt once said, "The best executive is the one who has sense enough to pick good men to do what he wants done, and self-restraint enough to keep from meddling with them while they do it."

However, let it be known that freedom of movement does not imply freedom from accountability.

Be prepared for possible mistakes. And when they come, never turn your back on them. Find out what went wrong and, most importantly, why. But the emphasis should be on building up, rather than tearing down, the person's confidence. Advance preparation for possible mistakes will help you to cope constructively with them when they occur. It goes without saying that if mistakes occur too often, more drastic action may be called for. This may mean that the work was not turned over properly or that you delegated to the wrong person. Be ready to correct either situation.

Maintain overall control. A common mistake is the turning over of total responsibility *and* control along with the assignment. As long as you remain the individual's immediate superior, final authority should remain in your hands. Whenever I delegate to individuals or committees, I follow up with a memo and spell out what I have said. I keep a copy and tell my secretary to bring it to my attention at a certain date, so that I can check the progress. Delegation is *not* abdication. The memo and the copy make sure that whatever was delegated *will happen.*

A sound supervisor-subordinate relationship is the only framework within which effective delegation can take place. If this relationship exists, the administrator will know the individual's interests and potential, will have that person's confidence, and they will be in constant communication.

A key word in the delegation process is the word *entrust.* When you delegate, you entrust the entire matter to the other person along with sufficient authority to make necessary decisions. This is quite a different thing from saying, "Just do what I tell you to do." In an entrusting situation an employee and the administrator are ready for the delegation process, and they can practice it for the benefit of themselves and the entire organization.

When I find myself trying to do more than I can handle, *the work cascades on me.* That's when I go out and play golf, or just get out of the office. There is really very little I do that someone else can't. I just need to give them an opportunity.

Do you need to give someone an opportunity? In my book, *The Making of a Christian Leader* (pp. 166–69), there are four pages of questions that will assist you in your moving toward good delegation, such as:

- Do you have to take work home almost every night?
- Do you need two or more telephones to keep up with the job?
- Do you have unfinished jobs accumulating, or difficulty meeting deadlines?
- Are you inclined to keep a finger on everything that is going on?
- Do you hesitate to admit that you need help to keep on top of your job?

This then is the much-discussed and much-misused art of delegation. One administrator likened his working day to a time bank. "When I delegate," he said, "I make a deposit of minutes, so that I may make a subsequent withdrawal of hours." This becomes the priceless gift received through effective delegation.

How Well
Are You Motivated?

Richard LeTourneau, son of R. G. LeTourneau, American industrialist and construction machinery giant, in his book *Management Plus*, says:

> I personally do not have that natural abounding energy and drive I often see in others. My enthusiasm has to be pumped up; and I guess it bothered me over the years to see my dad go at a pace nearly twice my capacity, even though he was nearly forty years older than I. For this reason particularly I have given a great deal of study to this matter of motivation and drive. I wanted to find out how I could develop my own. It certainly isn't easy to do, I can tell you that. But it can be done with the proper goals in life and the sustaining power available from God.

I agree with LeTourneau that to become a motivated person and to motivate others is not an easy task. But regardless of who you are and what your occupation is—pastor, small businessman, high school teacher—every believer can become a motivated person and can develop the ability to motivate others.

To motivate others is to infuse in people a spirit of eagerness to perform effectively. As you discipline yourself to become a motivated person, others will be inspired through your example and the work you do.

Means of Motivation

Motivation, then, is the work an administrator performs to get people to do what has to be done. The late J. C. Penney called it, "Getting things done through other people." Let's look at some of the various means of motivation.

Encouragement. Most often an administrator motivates through encouragement, or inspiration. However, too often this type of motivation is thought of only in relation to our subordinates. We have no difficulty recognizing our accountability for motivating those who report to us. But motivation is something that should occur not only down the line, but also across and up. We are apt to overlook our obligation to inspire and encourage other administrators at our own level as well as our superiors.

Participation. When peer administrators or our boss fail to take certain steps or to perform work that should have been done on our behalf, don't retire into your shell or allow frustration to consume you; rather, utilize the motivating tools of participation and communication in a way that will awaken their interest and energize them to take necessary action.

Recognition. Recognition should also be practiced in these areas. When another administrator does something well that relates to your responsibilities, a sincere and honest compliment will help motivate that person to accomplish other good work on your behalf.

I have long had a program of sending birthday cards to my associates and colleagues in World Vision. It never ceases to amaze me how much appreciated this simple gesture is. I'll often get a thank-you note from the recipient.

Remember, too, that the boss himself is the one who usually

works "in the kitchen." He ladles out recognition, but rarely receives it. My heart is so warmed when someone who works in our organization sends me a note of appreciation . . . or gives a cheery word of affirmation as I walk through our buildings to greet our staff. They perhaps don't realize how this motivates me to do *more* for and with them. No matter how brief, every note of recognition is meaningful.

Praise. Appropriate praise is like sunshine to the human spirit. People cannot flower and grow without it. As wise a man as Solomon spoke on this principle. "A word spoken in due season, how good it is" (Prov. 15:23).

Coercion. There will, of course, be situations that will require a more forceful motivating action. Some experts use the term "coercion" as a motivating word.

This is an area where I believe a Christian administrator needs to be individually led by the Holy Spirit; coercion is something the pharaohs and the Roman emperors used. They possessed the necessary power; all they required were enough slaves and whips. When one has been given power, regardless of its nature, it becomes easier not to feel a need to deal in courteous and understanding ways.

The administrator who is led by the Spirit of God will rarely resort to the use of secular power to motivate. He can be firm in his dealings without being harsh or unkind.

Self-motivation

You can't create self-motivation *in* other people. You *can* create a set of circumstances that might lead to motivation; but the desire for it and the creation of it must come from within the individual. You've got to know how to handle people, how to motivate them, how to get them to do the things you want them to do, *because they want to do them.*

Difficult? I should say so. That's why John D. Rockefeller

once said, "I will pay more for the ability to deal with people than for any other ability under the sun." I certainly agree. Willing workers are fairly easy to find. But internally motivated leaders who have developed the ability to size up and to motivate others are not easy to come by.

This sizing-up/motivating is an art in itself. Some people need a reward or stroking in order to finish a job. I may simply suggest the same task to another person and it will be done. Still others require pushing to accomplish the same task. My responsibility as a motivator is to stimulate people to do what has to be done, by whatever means. I strive to stimulate employees through praise, approval, and help; and I seldom need to incite action by other means.

I believe the most effective motivation is self-motivation. If we can get people to work *because they want to*—not because they are driven to do it—we will secure the most effective and enduring performance. How is this accomplished? Here is what works for me:

First, I seek to be a *model* for my staff. When I am in town I am in my office every morning before 8:00 A.M. I want people to see that the requirement of promptness for them is also important to me. I don't care so much when my supervisors quit for the day, but I *do care* when they start in the morning. The getting up and getting to work on time comes from more than the desire to put bread on the table. It comes from a desire to be productive.

Second, I am personally motivated because I want to be productive, because I have to *give account* of my time when I stand before the Lord. Jesus said that I should not fear "those who kill the body. . . . But rather fear Him who is able to destroy both soul and body in hell" (Matt. 10:28). And the Lord has told me to "redeem the time" (Col. 4:5).

Third, I am also motivated by *goals*. Outside of my obedience to God's command to redeem the time, nothing motivates me personally more than goals.

My friend John W. Alexander, in his book *Managing Our Work*, says:

> Occasionally it is said that a leader must choose between people-centered and goal-centered, the implication being that the two are mutually exclusive. Our philosophy of goal-setting is based on the premise that the two are not in contradiction and that a leader who loves people and is a good manager can be both people- and goal-centered.
>
> Every leader should have two sets of objectives, goals, and standards: one for himself as a person and one for the team which he leads (his local church, Sunday school class, company, student group, cell group, area team, department team, etc.).
>
> Within an organization, construction of annual and long-range plans should begin at the top. Let the chief executive first construct his own goals and standards and circulate copies throughout the movement so that any person who desires to study them has opportunity to do so. A person is more likely to participate if he sees his supervisor working according to goals and standards. One worker, after completing his first set of goals, wrote his area director, "I cannot say I'm sorry to have them finished, but I certainly am glad that God changed my attitude about it all. Will you be sure to pass on (to the president) how much his own goals helped me understand for the first time just what goals are? Thanks."

Fourth, I am motivated when new *records are set*, new heights are reached. Psychiatrist Ari Kiev has described this process well in a speech to psychology students a few years ago:

> Observing the lives of people who have mastered adversity, I have repeatedly noted that they have established goals and, irrespective of obstacles, sought with all their effort to achieve

them. From the moment they've fixed an objective in their mind and decided to concentrate all their energies on a specific goal, they begin to surmount the most difficult odds.

Let me illustrate this with a well-known sports fact. For years the four-minute mile was considered beyond man's physical capabilities. Thousands of athletes regularly attempted to break this limitation, but it seemed that it just couldn't be done. Then one day an athlete who refused to believe it couldn't be done did it.

But the amazing thing is *not* what he did. It is what other athletes were able to do after this psychological barrier had been removed. Within five years after that, the four-minute-mile barrier had been broken by *21 different runners 50 different times!* And within fifteen years 107 runners had broken the record 320 times!

Christian administrators should be aware of the flip side of this peculiar phenomenon, for it can develop in our own personal lives as well as in our administration. Rather than overcoming obstacles to set new records, we may place imaginary limitations on ourselves. Because we dwell upon these imaginary limitations, they become very real—actual physical limitations. This is because our mind has told our body it can't be done; therefore, *it really can't be done.*

In my own life, when the thought "can't be done" comes surging into my mind, I have found that if I put into action a twofold plan, those nonproductive thoughts will be driven out and replaced with "I can do all things through Christ."

Part One of my twofold plan is to remind myself that God has created me in His own image—a creature designed to take dominion over this world and all that is in it, a creature designed to create just as God creates. And how does God create? With words. So then, with words, I begin to say out loud, "God said I *can do* all things. Therefore, for this project, *I can do it.* So with God's help, it's now up to me to learn how I can do it."

In Part Two I plan small increments of action that will allow me *to begin doing* whatever it is that can't be done. I begin chipping away at it.

In our work at World Vision it seems that we are constantly faced with impossible challenges and projects. How, for example, does one go about taking care of a refugee camp, Las Dhure, in Somalia, East Africa, with 76,000 desperately needy and suffering people? This is a typical challenge we face. The answer, given to us by Bob Pierce in our early days, is "one at a time." "Simply because you can't help everybody," he would say, "doesn't mean you can't help somebody."

Whatever the degree of the administrative gift you possess, you can learn to be a motivator. Begin by being a pacesetter for those around you; develop your self-motivation first. Then learn to reach out to others in ways that will increase their motivation.

The Administrator as an Active Planner

I believe the Scriptures teach that God is the great Master Planner who laid out a path for all human history even before the earth existed (see Eph. 1:9–10). And throughout the Bible God has revealed His interest in plans—both His and mine.

In Proverbs 16:3 He says, "Roll your works upon the Lord—commit and trust them wholly to Him; [He will cause your thoughts to become agreeable to His will, and] *so shall your plans to be established and succeed*" (*Amplified Bible*, italics added).

And again in Proverbs 16:9, "A man's mind plans his way, but the Lord directs his steps and makes them sure" (*Amplified Bible*).

93

The above Scriptures cover the plans we make for ourselves. But Jeremiah 29:11 concerns the plans that God Himself has for His children. "For I know the plans *I have for you*, says the Lord. They are plans for good and not for evil, to give you a future and a hope" (TLB, italics added). God's plans for us are also evident in these words in Isaiah 14:24: "The Lord of hosts has sworn, saying, Surely as I have thought and planned, so shall it come to pass; and as I have purposed, so shall it stand" (*Amplified Bible*).

Planning Is a Process

As administrators, there are many different ways of displaying our plans. It doesn't matter what method you use; the important thing is to make sure they are displayed and to keep them before you continuously. It is also important to make sure individuals who will be fitting into those plans understand clearly exactly what their role is and how those plans will impact them.

We need to see that planning is a continuous process. It begins before the "acting," then continues alongside the doing of the project. It is helpful to think of planning as acting, evaluating, and replanning.

Christian organizations have a singular advantage over secular organizations in that they can anticipate and plan for a high degree of goal ownership. Secularly, the primary motivational goal is very often that of earning money. Such is generally not the case with Christian organizations where the most powerful motivational force and goal is that of bringing glory to Jesus Christ. Whereas with a secular organization the members may not be single-minded with management in the attainment of profit, this is not so with the Christian organization. There, the professed goal of each individual is the accomplishment of the single, stated aim.

Participatory Planning

What many organizations do not realize is that planning can be a very useful way of involving many people in considerable depth. It ties directly into motivating people. The act of asking individuals or groups to consider alternate or optimum ways of reaching their goal, or the act of asking them to propose specific goals against the higher purpose of the organization, can be the trigger for a whole series of events. It can not only give people a feeling of having participated in the organization, but it can stimulate a host of new ideas. This is just as true for the local church as it is for the Christian organization which uses no volunteers.

Participation in planning has a powerful motivational impact. Motivation to accomplish results tends to increase as people are given opportunity to participate in the decisions affecting those results.

Participation involves making systematic provision for consultation with subordinates in those matters directly related to their jobs. In developing participation, an administrator asks subordinates for their suggestions, recommendations, and advice in matters that affect their work. Psychologically, the administrator develops *mutuality of interest.*

Motivation to accomplish results tends to increase as people are informed about matters affecting those results. Let your people know when plans you have made together are fulfilled. The more a person knows about a matter, the more interest and concern he will develop. When an administrator makes an obvious effort to keep people informed of his plans, he is telling them, "I think you are important. I want to be sure you know what is going on." If he withholds information, he makes it quite clear that he feels it is of little importance whether or not his people know what is occurring. Being informed helps give meaning to the job.

It is much more satisfying to sit up front in the driver's seat where you know about things that are happening than to be perched in a rear seat where you get only sporadic and fragmentary glimpses of what is going on. If we know what the goals are and what progress is being made toward them, it is not difficult to feel a real and vital part of the team.

In our ministry at World Vision we seek to have our various departments have regular "days away" on "information retreats." It has become a spiritual exercise and challenge. We explain what we are doing—and why. We show how each person's role is vitally important in the project. Every time it happens staff morale measurably rises!

People want to feel that they are part of the team. They want to be accepted and appreciated by their fellows. The greater this team feeling, the more strongly they will feel impelled to work hard and productively to achieve the goals of the group.

Side Benefits of Careful Planning

Planning is so important in today's world that it occupies a major time apportionment of some of the world's most respected businessmen. And apparently Jesus considered planning to be important also, because He spoke of planning in the parable of the unjust steward. When the man's master called the steward to account for his handling of company goods and accounts, the steward carefully planned how he would protect his own interests when he left the employ of the company.

When the top administrator learned of the employee's actions, Jesus said of him that "the master commended the unjust steward because he had dealt [planned] shrewdly." Jesus concluded this portion of the parable with these words, "For the sons of this world are more shrewd in their generation than the sons of light" (Luke 16:8).

In this context, it is clear that neither Jesus nor the administrator of whom He spoke commended the steward *for his actions*. Rather, they commended the steward for his wisdom in planning ahead, then executing his plans.

What are some of the side-benefits of responsible planning? *Successful leaders have found that planning allows us to master change.* Planning forces us to organize our expectations and develop a program to bring them about. It is a most effective way to draw out the best in all of us—our best thinking, our best interests and aims—and to enable us to develop the most efficient way of achieving our maximum growth.

Planning forces accountability. And everyone needs to be accountable, not just to God, but to another human being. As a man who attended one of our time management seminars said: "I used to feel it was so unnecessary to write detailed goals and standards; but now I can see that through them needed changes in my own life, as well as direction in staff work, have become a reality. The standards for measuring myself are no longer burdensome; they are incentives to achieve new challenges."

Planning is the intellectual arm of organized growth. It is the prologue to tomorrow. And yet it should not be the activity of the few, because it is really the business of us all.

Personally, I plan by constantly making goals: short-term goals, intermediate goals, long-term goals, lifetime goals, goals for today, goals for this year, this month, this week, *today*. If I don't review those goals, it's easy to slip back. For years I have had six carefully prayed-for lifetime goals that I keep typed on a card in my wallet, which I review about every six months.

I review my week's goals at the beginning of the week. On Monday morning I write down what I want to accomplish during the week. Then each morning that I am in the office, I talk with my secretary about the goals for that day, the things we want to accomplish. It's a process. I don't think, "Now, I'm going to sit down and talk about goals." It just becomes an automatic thinking-through process, like driving a car. When you are first learning, you have to be conscious of every step; but after practice it becomes a part of your automatic behavior.

Let me illustrate. The publisher and I set a goal for the completion of this book. We realized that it might become necessary to reevaluate our target date; but to begin with we set a specific date for the book's completion. Had we not set a deadline, but merely talked about how nice it would be to write this book and that we surely would do it when there was extra time—then the writing of it would have dragged on for a long time. Possibly it would have never gotten done.

Goals, of course, are not always reached. But they almost always can be reset if they are not reached. This is what an airline pilot would call "in-flight course corrections."

Some studies that have come out of Cornell Medical Center attest to the fact that goals are one of the most powerful motivating forces known to man. One of the Medical Center's psychiatrists, Dr. Ari Kiev, states, "With goals people can overcome confusion and conflict over incompatible values, contradictory desires, and frustrated relationships with friends and relatives, all of which often result from the absence of rational life strategies."

Don't Overplan

Remember that effective planning is incomplete planning. Don't overplan. It tends to inhibit people's creativity and eliminate a sense of participation; it fails to take into account the fact that things will change. Rather, we should see that the very open-endedness of plans will keep people alert to the fact that they have to be continually planning.

Planning, as we said, is a process. This means that we should be careful not to plan beyond our ability. By this we mean that if the planning process is new to your organization, don't try to cover everything. Gain experience as you go along. To be a detailed planner you have to first learn to be a general planner.

The function of planning is the work an administrator performs to predetermine a course of action.

Forecast Planning

Planning is so vital, it is one of the most important administrative functions. I believe the ability to project oneself into the future is the essence of planning. We can do this through setting objectives, forecasting or identifying some key conditions or assumptions, and determining the course of future action and policies.

My definition of forecast planning includes: (1) establishing and interpreting goals and objectives; (2) formulating and issuing policies which are, in effect, standing management decisions; (3) establishing programs, then functions and activities to be pursued in reaching the goals which have been decided upon; (4) differentiating between short- and long-range plans, between standing plans and interim plans.

While I am at it, let me offer a few more definitions. I would define "forecasting" as the work an administrator performs to estimate the future. By "establishing objectives" I mean the work an administrator performs to determine the *end results* to be accomplished. "Establishing procedures," on the other hand, is the work an administrator performs to develop and apply standardized methods of performing specific work—how you get to where you want to go. And "developing policies" is the work a manager performs to outline and interpret standing decisions that apply to repetitive questions and problems of significance to the enterprise as a whole.

I have found that one of the vital kinds of work required of an administrator is that of doing everything within his command to help his followers and himself create the kind of future they want.

Getting Things Done

If results are to be accomplished, action must be taken. There are two basic ways of getting things done. The first is to plunge ahead, doing the things that appear to be necessary, handling problems as they come up, and taking advantage of opportunities as they occur. This approach may be successful, but it generally requires an extremely capable individual who will be able to mastermind everything that must be done as the process moves along. If he can be alert to the needs of everyone and make the decisions required to keep the whole enterprise moving, his leadership will be effective.

Even if we were to find such an individual, however, we would discover that the work and the problems would eventually become too large and too complex for any one person. It is here that the alternative becomes important. This involves thinking through, in advance, both what we want to accomplish and how it might best be accomplished. Essentially, a plan is a mental picture of future accomplishment. It helps us get the job accomplished in several ways.

1. When we plan, we take time to reflect and analyze, to consider alternatives, to *make sound, considered decisions* about the future. We decide in advance what we are going to do, how we will do it, under what conditions we will carry it out, how we will accomplish it, and what we will require to get the results we want. Do be careful here; having the gift of administration in no way guarantees good planning. It is through disciplining ourselves to think ahead that we avoid the tendency to make hasty judgments and to take haphazard action.

2. Proper planning greatly *simplifies the task* of an administrator. It makes integrated and coordinated effort possible. If we know where we are going, we are much more likely to get there. Once we have the whole picture in mind, it is easier to

make the parts fit together and to ensure that the action that follows is timed so it will take place in the proper sequence.

3. Planning *enables us to make the most effective and economical use of our assets*—manpower, equipment, facilities, and money. If we identify in advance our needs for people, we can develop individuals inside the organization so that they will be ready when the opportunity for promotion appears.

Planning makes it possible to let subordinates know what is required of them and to give them an opportunity to participate in the decisions that are made. This keeps interest and enthusiasm at a high level and enables the manager to incorporate into his plans the best thinking of those closest to the point where the action will be carried out.

The importance of planning is highlighted by the emphasis well-managed companies put upon it. Industry leaders, convinced that their future success depends as much upon the thought their administrators give to planning as to process and technology, expect administrators at all levels, from first-line supervisor to top executive, to devote a substantial portion of their time to planning before taking action.

During a train trip the renowned jurist, Oliver Wendell Holmes, was unable to locate his ticket when the conductor asked for it. After watching Holmes fumble through his pockets in growing dismay, the conductor said, "That's all right, Mr. Holmes. I'm sure you have your ticket somewhere. If you don't find it until you've gotten off, just mail it to us when you get home. We'll certainly trust you."

Holmes replied, "Young man, my problem isn't to find my ticket. It's to find out where I'm going!"

Too many administrators have such lack of clarity in common with the distinguished Supreme Court justice. All too often, some of us don't have the foggiest idea of where we are or where our organizations are going. This unawareness can be catastrophic. And to some organizations it has been. That's why I believe that intensive planning for the future, determining where you are going, is an indispensable element of effective administration.

A few planning ideas that I have found useful come from some statements on the subject by my friend David Secunda, who is vice-president of the American Management Association. He says:

Some define planning as the best of the management functions to close the gap between what we are doing and what we want to accomplish. To others, planners are "hunchers equipped with numbers" and sworn changers of mere chance and extrapolation. The future attracts their attention and, through a keen identification of key assumptions, the organization is provided with steadiness, if not confidence. Change is not avoided, but possibly created and always managed. All agree it's the winners' way to deal with complex, confused, and changing conditions to minimize crisis management and its preoccupation with surprises. Some helpful notes of executive planners follows:

1. A broad-based, well-understood sense of direction is the key to effective long-range planning. (Remember, there is nothing magic about "five years.")

2. When planning is chiefly a numbers game, it doesn't work. Technique and approach are more important than quantitative numbers. Critical assumptions influencing major ingredients of your business in the future should take priority.

3. Developing a strategy shapes a company by implementing itself in the allocation of discretionary resources.

4. If choices are not made among identifiable alternatives, we must live with ambiguity and can rationalize ourselves into hopelessness.

5. What we should do next should have some relationship with what we do ultimately, and it is not wise to plan beyond our vision.

6. The people at the bottom like to get some options from the

top to inject excitement into what they are part of, even though executives too high up tend to forget where the battle is really being fought.

7. Planning must be placed more in the hands of executors—those who accomplish—and less in the hands of designers. Eliminate issues that do not lead to actions.

8. The results of the process of planning—apart from the process—must be highlighted. Merely having a plan doesn't make it happen.

Goals, Priorities, and Planning

This chapter has been a restatement of my belief that planning in general and goal-setting in particular are good in theory and useful in practice in both kingdoms. Those of you who are still skeptical about the whole process, however, will need to actually experience the benefits of setting and realizing goals before you will become convinced of the importance of planning. Those of you who want specific outlines and charts to assist you in learning how to plan in a more productive manner may find the book *Strategy for Living*, by Edward Dayton and myself, useful. It is written in a practical, how-to style and deals basically with goals, priorities, and planning.

It's very easy for goals just to limit themselves to daydreams. "Someday I will . . ." can become a fantasy that never becomes a reality. In order to make your goal operational, you need a way to accomplish it. You need a plan. And a deadline.

It is not a question of whether we will or will not plan. To make no plans is a plan in itself. Rather, it is a question of whether we will affect the future with purpose or at random. "The new man . . . is out to learn what he ought to be, according to the plan of God" (Col. 3:10 author's paraphrase). We who administrate have a responsibility to decide what God wants us to be and what He wants us to do, and therefore we have a responsibility to plan.

And as you make your plans within God's plan, "I pray that your hearts will be flooded with light so that you can see something of the future he has called you to share. . . . I pray that you will begin to understand how incredibly great his power is to help those who believe him" (Eph. 1:18–19 TLB). With this light and this power, you too can have that wisdom from God that causes "your thoughts to become agreeable to His will, and so shall your plans be established and succeed" (Prov. 16:3 *Amplified Bible*).

Administrating through Communication

Communication has been defined as the use of language and signs, the transmission of information, and as a means of influencing behavior. This is a good beginning definition, but there is more. For when we communicate, we want to do more than use signs and symbols or transmit information; we desire more even than to influence behavior.

Beyond Transmitting Knowledge

If we give someone instructions, we are not satisfied just to speak words to ensure they are heard, or even to cause the other person to act. We want the other person *to do* what we intended in *the way we intended* it to be done. In other words, we want the other person to understand what we want done, the way we understand it. Therefore, the end result of communication is understanding; and there is a great difference between knowing something and understanding it.

In the context of this book, it is my desire to discuss communicating as the work an administrator performs to create understanding. Mental and physical effort must be exerted to communicate effectively. From the standpoint of the administrator, it must result in comprehension—the sharing of the same meaning—or it is not true communication.

Let me illustrate with the classic story of the man whose car had stalled. Another car stopped and the driver asked if she could assist him.

"Yes, I'd appreciate a push."

"I'll be glad to do that," she answered.

He said, "I've got automatic transmission and you'll have to get me moving at thirty miles an hour before the engine will start."

She nodded her agreement. He got behind the wheel in preparation for the push. He looked in his rear-view mirror and, to his absolute horror, he noted that she had backed her car up half a block and was now bearing down on him right at thirty miles an hour!

Obviously something was lacking in communication.

Some administrators look upon communication as a one-way process—telling. Telling others what they want them to know, what they want them to think, and what they want them to do. And by such a definition, they believe they are communicating.

Communication rarely breaks down for lack of our desire to communicate. Most of us want to be understood, often desperately so. But we may find it difficult to cut through the cloud of misunderstanding that often seems to block us from making effective contact with another person. One reason we fail to make ourselves understood is because we frequently mistake the vehicle we use for communicating with the communication itself.

Why do we so commonly mistake the form of the communication for the communication itself? Think of the word "communication." What do you associate with it? Perhaps a telephone, someone speaking, or even a memo. In this frame of reference if we perceive the need to improve communication, we would then look to the installation of more and better telephones, of more and better talking, of more and better memos. We may take it for granted that the letters we send, the bulletins we put up, or the memos we circulate are communications in themselves. This is like assuming that you are giving a guest dinner by letting him observe a steak on a platter, when in actuality he has to eat and digest it before it really becomes his.

Beyond Transmitting Feelings

Communication sometimes fails because, as administrators, we are too concerned with getting other people to understand *us*—what we want and how we feel. Since we are accustomed to giving commands, we tend to think that others have an obligation to understand us and will work hard to do so. The contrary is more often the case. Effective communication begins with understanding what the other person wants and needs.

Difficult as this work may seem, the effectiveness of an administrator rests in large measure upon that person's skill to communicate. Plans can be acted upon, organization can be made more effective, motivation can take place, and controls can be exercised only if we can convey our meaning about these things to others—and understand what they are trying to convey to us.

I'm a strong believer in personal contact, especially in employee relations. Through my years at World Vision, I have learned to know a high percentage of our people on a first-name basis. And the better I get to know them, the better I am able to communicate with them.

A cheery "good morning" is not enough. Neither is an infrequent pat on the back. Nor can an administrator forget about employees all year long, then expect to win their confidence during the camaraderie of the annual picnic. To truly communicate with our employees and colleagues, we must take a genuine interest in them. We must let them know continually that their contributions are vital to our common effort, and we must reaffirm our common bond as coworkers with Jesus Christ.

For many years now we have had day-long retreats for our staff members. We now have so many on our staff that we must divide the group and have four, five, even six of these retreats every year. We take our colleagues away to a nice place for our meetings, provide a lovely luncheon for them, and simply share together what God is doing in our lives and in our work. This is not primarily for training, or even for information, but it is an excellent opportunity for our leadership and the staff to get to know each other in a more intimate way.

Everyone in attendance is encouraged to participate in smaller groups that we set up. We provide exercises where each person shares and is heard. Such situations as "If I were leading World Vision, I would . . ." or "I wish World Vision would . . ." are posited, so our people have the opportunity to express their interests and concerns for our ministry.

We have repeatedly found that these annual retreats are some of the finest things we do to build camaraderie and a high sense of morale within the organization.

Six Key Questions

I believe I do a better job communicating when I thoughtfully review the following six questions. The first three apply to me:

(1) What do I *intend* to say or write?

(2) What do I *in reality* say or write, sometimes in spite of my good intentions?

(3) What will be the emotional *impact* upon the recipient of what I say or write?

The other three questions apply to the person(s) with whom I desire to communicate:

(1) What does the person *expect* to hear or read?

(2) What will the person *actually* read or hear, at times despite what is actually spoken or written?

(3) How will the person *feel* about what is read or heard?

The administrator must bear in mind that the purpose is not to impress, but to communicate; not to carry on a semantic handball game, but to get through to the other person. Accordingly, the task is: (a) to translate what is significant to him so that it will be acceptable to the receiver, because if it is not acceptable the message could well be rejected; (b) to translate what is important to him so that it is meaningful to the receiver, on the receiver's terms rather than on those of the communicator; (c) to translate what is significant to the communicator into terms that will have the impact he seeks on the receiver. If those three conditions are not met, then the communication will at best be limited, at worst nil.

Regardless of the authority or status of the communicator, it is essential that he take for granted that he is more the servant than the master of his people. He may dictate the goals, but the receiver dictates the kind of communication to which he will respond positively.

God, of course, is the ultimate Communicator; and we would do well to attempt to pattern our communications after His. When man failed to heed one method, God used another in order to better get His message across. For example, when man refused to regard God's message in the Garden of Eden, God didn't give up.

Instead, He sought for another man who would listen and obey, this time Abraham. Again, His people listened and heeded His instructions for a time, then backed off.

God spoke again and again—through Moses and the prophets. Finally, God gave mankind the perfect communication—He gave Himself. He modeled His message and plan through the Person of His Son; and in so doing, He both spoke and demonstrated His desires.

Transmitting Beyond Words

Human communication involves far more than most of us are aware of, including how we sit, the gestures we use, how we dress, even the amount of space we need around us.

Body language, or kinesics. Kinesics comes from the Greek word *kinēsis*, meaning "motion." It describes the communication that comes from every part of a person. Some psychologists say kinesics is so important that the emotional impact of any message is 55 percent facial and body, 38 percent vocal intonation, and only 7 percent verbal, or pure word usage. This means our bodies sometimes talk louder than our mouths. It also means that if our bodies are contradicting our words, those with whom we are trying to communicate are going to find it difficult to understand or believe our words. In a way, it's like fish swimming in a sea of signals. We send and receive many of these signals without consciously realizing we are communicating.

Clothing. What we wear makes a statement of some kind. Every time we dress, we make choices about the way we want to appear. Even an "I-don't-care" message is a clear statement. Our clothing affects our own mood as well as the moods of our colleagues.

The kind of clothing we wear is important in other ways. It influences our posture and movement; it serves either to animate or slow us down. The administrator who shows up for work wearing a Beethoven sweatshirt and sandals is certainly communicating something, although he may not do so for long. The kind of communication that is likely to take place between a man in bathing trunks and another in formal dress will be quite different from the communication that would take place if both were dressed alike.

Society is aware of this principle and uses clothing to help enforce its rules. The dress codes of restaurants and schools are intended to control behavior as much as to control appearance.

A friend of mine who served as a member of a public school board told how they experimented with a stricter, more formal dress code. At first only the teachers participated, and the discipline problems decreased to a slight degree. Then they imposed a mandatory dress code upon the students and discipline problems decreased dramatically.

At our offices we have a dress code for all employees in which we state:

> As a leader in the Christian community, World Vision is looked upon as an example in our field. Our organization is involved in an aspect of public relations, since public tours are given of the facilities daily. Therefore, we need to bear in mind at all times that our dress, as well as our manner and personal conduct, must consistently be reflective of Christ in us as a witness.
>
> We request our personnel to dress with good taste and modesty. Our dress is to be moderate, unpretentious, and thoughtfully chosen to avoid anything that might debase or cheapen. The key biblical words governing the dress of Christians are found in Paul's first letter to Timothy, chapter two, verse nine:
>
> "Modest"—virtuous, honorable, respectable.
>
> "Decent"—reverent, modest, respectful.
>
> "Proper"—moderation which does not overstep stated limits.

Environment. Another influential area of communication is environment. Every person who walks into your office receives a message before you have said one word. A room is pleasant or unpleasant, invigorating or relaxing, authoritarian or intimate, disciplined or casual, depending on our sensory reactions to it.

I have sought to arrange my office in such a way as to utilize these subtleties to the best advantage. For example, both my office furniture and arrangements lend themselves to either a formal business setting or one that is conversational and inviting.

When the more formal mode is needed, I generally sit behind my desk, having the visitor sit opposite me. The message transmitted in this manner is, "Time is of the essence" or "Business only." For other occasions, I move from behind my desk and move closer to my visitor, in a chair or on the couch, thus indicating, "I'm here to listen" or "to visit," and time is not necessarily a pressing factor.

Recently I spent a most enjoyable hour with my friend Oral Roberts in his study in Tulsa, Oklahoma, and I was most agreeably impressed by the way he put me completely at ease. He served me a cup of tea, invited me to sit at one end of a comfortable couch, while he sat on the other. Within seconds we had established rapport—because of his graciousness *and* the informal setting.

Administrators must learn how they can arrange their offices so they can inject the proper atmosphere into any conference or meeting at a moment's notice in order to achieve the desired result.

The following chart is one a friend of mine uses in communications seminars. You may find it useful for evaluating your own office.

It is not the intent of this book to define patterns and meanings of body language and physical environment; but rather to make us aware of these dimensions of communication and to suggest research on the subjects if additional information is desired.

It's a Two-Way Street

Because communication is a form of influence, it does not involve a unilateral bludgeoning, with one person active and the other passive, but rather a relationship in which both parties play distinct but complementary roles. It is a relationship in which the communicator controls only half of the transaction,

Office items	What I Want These Items to Say about Me	What These Items Really Say to Others

with the receiver probably controlling the more important half. It is a form of interaction to which the recipient often brings as much as, or more than, the communicator.

The communicator and receiver both hear and see subjectively and selectively. So the important and the incidental topics are determined not by logic alone, but rather by a curious mix of cognitive and emotional factors.

It is common knowledge that people tend to magnify what is pleasing and to block out what is unpleasant. The communicator must seek to determine in advance just what elements of an interaction are likely to be magnified beyond the limits intended and which might be glossed over or ignored.

A way of seeing and hearing is at the same time a way of *not* seeing and hearing. This applies with equal weight to sender and receiver. The two tendencies in combination inevitably produce tunnel vision for both parties. The administrator focuses on what is significant to him, but realizes that his job is to communicate it in such a way that the recipient will have the same understanding of it.

A receiver of a communication usually has two questions: (1) What's in the communication for me? (2) How will it affect me? If possible, therefore, the communication should contain something of value to the receiver. The natural human tendency is for all people to be self-centered. Jesus made reference to this natural tendency when He commanded us to love our neighbor as we love ourselves (see Matt. 19:19).

A person more readily accepts changes in procedures if the advantages for him are pointed out. He executes orders more effectively if the reasons for them are explained. He finds discipline less distasteful if he not only knows *why* he is being chewed out, but is also aware of the benefits that can accrue to him if he alters his behavior.

Three Helpful Words

Another valuable aid to the prevention of misunderstanding is for the communicator to take advantage of the subtleties of the similarities and differences between the words *common, community*, and *communion*. This is helpful, because what the communicator and the receiver have in *common* automatically both defines the areas of possible communication *and* sets up the limits within which it must take place. Where there is little in common, there can be little communication.

Community refers to shared objectives, values, interests, and attitudes. Where there is no sense of community, attempts to interact are often futile. This is as true of relationships between administrators and subordinates as it is between teachers and students, husbands and wives, or the governments of Russia and the United States.

Communion means a mutual intercourse. There is fellowship in communion. In 2 Corinthians 6:14 we are admonished, "Do not be unequally yoked together with unbelievers. For what fellowship has righteousness with lawlessness? And what communion has light with darkness?"

Communication in the purest sense of the word cannot take place without commonality, community, and fellowship.

The Listening Administrator

Administrators are people who spend the largest percentage of their time in some form of communication, including listening. It is a sad indictment that many administrators engage in what we call "marginal listening," which involves little more than sporadic attentive hearing. An example would be doing an expense report during a telephone call.

Others engage in "evaluative listening"—listening with the fists clenched; listening in order to disagree with, rebut, or shoot down the communicator. Every administrator should show his employee the courtesy of listening to what he has to say, even though he may disagree or find it somewhat distasteful.

The following suggestions have been of assistance to me in listening projectively and putting myself in the speaker's frame of reference.

Pay complete attention. The average hearing speed is four to six times speaking speed. Distraction and woolgathering are ever present dangers. If the listener does not give complete attention to the speaker, a great deal of the message will be lost.

But there is more to listening than mental attentiveness. One must listen with the *whole being.* I have earlier mentioned that facial expressions, gestures, and posture all play a part in the process. No one is going to talk for long to an unresponsive, stony face. A smile, a "uh-huh," or even a "mmh" reassures the other party that the administrator is still attending to the message.

Listen for the real message. The listening process is like the X-ray process. It cuts through skin, muscle, and bone to get to the object it is aimed at. The listener X-rays through the words and even the silences of the speaker to come to grips with the true message. You might ask yourself, "Is the communication basically intellectual or is it emotional?" Be certain you are listening for meaning, not just being distracted by the words that convey the meaning. Are you aware of the connotations of the gestures and other elements of the transmission, or are you content to deal with the denotation of the words only?

Listen for what is not said. At times the real message is contained in the pauses, the silences, the omissions. Although the administrator is not expected to search for arcane meanings, reading between the lines is an essential skill.

Listen encouragingly. It is difficult at times to hold one's tongue. It takes self-discipline to let a person have his say without interruption. One aspect of this practice involves the charity of silence. The administrator should let some statements go by, rejecting the temptation to pour vinegar into an open wound, prove that the person is wrong, or make him feel inferior or inadequate.

The Scriptures tell us that Pilate marveled at Jesus because He kept silent. James tells us to be "slow to speak"(1:19). Paul says, "aspire to lead a quiet life" (1 Thess. 4:11). Isaiah assures us, "In quietness and confidence shall be your strength" (30:15). And Solomon wrote, "A soft answer turns away wrath" (Prov. 15:1).

Listen prudently. It is not necessary for the administrator to listen to everything that a person may want to say. In fact, at times he may have to prevent someone from baring his heart unduly. Saying too much today may cause almost irreparable embarrassment and bitterness tomorrow. A person under pressure natually tends to unburden himself when he feels that he has a sympathetic shoulder and an empathetic ear available. Take care not to take a pastoral role—unless, of course, you are one.

The administrator can protect both himself and the speaker by asking himself the following questions: (1) Is the matter job-related? (2) Is it within my authority and responsibility? (3) Is it within my area of competence? If the answers to these questions are negative, then a supportive referral should be made to other sources in or outside the organization that can cope with the difficulty, such as a Christian minister.

It is usually not wise to counsel regarding personal matters (finances, marriage, family, etc.) in a business discussion, even though the problem may be a very real one. I often suggest, when this occurs, that a separate time be set aside for a discussion or counseling session about the problem.

Listen to learn. The interchange should be a learning experience for both parties. The skillful listener can learn a great deal about the speaker. After all, every time a person speaks he reveals something of himself to the careful observer.

The listener can also learn something about himself by consciously observing his own behavior—noting his own reactions to attack, criticism, praise, flattery, and so on. He can learn a great deal as well about the relationship between himself and the speaker from how frank and candid the conversation becomes. Seek to determine to what extent either party feels a need to be defensive and what the sensitive areas are that one or the other tends to avoid—and why.

Administrators operate under a handicap when they listen only for what they *want* to hear. This means they have not learned to become good listeners, and therefore will not become good communicators. How many people do you know who make a decision first, then try to justify their reasoning?

They are the opinion-dodgers, people who have never learned to benefit from the stimulus of fresh ideas.

Speak with Clarity

Another guidepost for communicating effectively is clarity. A good guide for clarity in communication can be summed up in one word—understandability. Stay clear of high-sounding words and don't be afraid to use shirt-sleeves English. Call a road a road, not a "vehicular artery." In today's complex world, it is most helpful when we "defog" our language, when we speak in clear and simple terms.

One myth that has come down through the years is that a direct, simple explanation of serious or even profound matters is "talking down." On the contrary, talking down has to do with attitudes, not adverbs. We are not patronizing anyone when we put an idea in simple and vigorous words. To the contrary, it shows we are desirous of making our point quickly and clearly.

How do we achieve this clarity—the ability to speak and write straightforwardly? If we stop to remember that effective communication consists of relaying sharply defined ideas, the battle is half won. This means organizing our thoughts before we speak or write. In order to do this, we must first get the facts straight. Then we must arrange them in logical order. Finally, we must convey them clearly and concisely. This is perhaps the most difficult part.

By and large, those of us who want to communicate more effectively would do well to heed the advice of Rudolf Flesch, who admonishes us in his book *The Art of Plain Talk* to use:
- the familiar word in place of the unfamiliar.
- the concrete word in place of the abstract.
- the short word in place of the long.
- the single word in place of a circumlocution.

Words are precision instruments, and the right ones should be used for the purpose in hand. Are you in the habit of using the words "few," "some," or "many" when the precise meaning would be better conveyed by actual numbers and percentages? Do you check your terms for clarity?

Use the Listener's Language

I came across an article from *The Management Review* entitled "Memos That Get Across," by Pilson W. Kelly. He said:

> A source of obscurity is failure to operate in the language of all concerned. Don't write casually to lawyers about the redundant free transient in the grid circuit, nor to accountants about the pearlite in the left front finneganpin bearings, nor to engineers about obscure and far from evident sharp corners in the accounting system or in governmental procedure.

Communications, Kelly points out, are also blocked by special short-cut expressions peculiar to a restricted group. Thus, engineers have become accustomed to using "psi" for "pressure in pounds per square inch," but to most of the rest of us this is still a Greek letter.

In this connection, special idioms of the listener (or reader) should also be kept in mind. The British, for example, mean just the opposite from what we in America mean by the expression "tabling a matter." They mean, "Let's lay it on the table and discuss it now." Americans mean, "Let's put it off."

Sometimes we allow fuzziness to hinder our message because we want to use elegant expressions. Usually the short Anglo-Saxon words get ideas across much better than the longer and less familiar Latin-derived variety. A good rule to remember is: Use words which convey a vivid picture. Take this sentence for example: "The vehicle drew up before the edifice." There is no picture there. How much more concrete to say, "The mule pulled the cart to the front of the barn."

Words are vehicles for the transmission of ideas. Words take their meanings not from dictionary definitions, but rather from the semantic environments in which they are found. If this were not true, then "democracy" would have the same connotation for the Russian as for the American. The unwary administrator assumes that a superior, peer, or subordinate will attach the same meaning to a given word that he does. It is far wiser to think of words as containers. The content the communicator puts into the container is important; but even more important is the meaning the receiver takes out of the container.

A minister had just delivered a sermon of thanks for the generous donation that would enable the congregation to make the badly needed repairs to the village church. The donor of the funds, a man from a nearby city, was the honored guest that day. During the benedictory prayer, the minister was horrified when the guest rose and angrily stomped out of the church. Not until much later did he determine the reason.

In his prayer he had said, " . . . and Lord, we thank Thee for this succor." It was then that he realized that the millionaire had heard the sound of the word rather than the content. The word he had *heard* was far different from the word that was said. The result was a serious breakdown in communication!

Choose Your Words, Guard Your Lips

It is written in the Jewish Talmud that Torah (Bible) scholars were told:

> Be careful with your words. Exercise care in your choice of words, and do not make ambiguous statements that may be misunderstood or misconstrued. Always be careful to use the

clearest language possible. If you are in the habit of speaking in opaque, ambiguous terms, some people with little faith in God will read their own heresy into your words.

We must therefore be very cautious when we speak and not use code words, in-group language which could be misconstrued. Use such unambiguous language that even your most antagonistic opponent will not be able to use your words to mislead others.

We can never be too careful with our word choices. Words are the most powerful things in the universe. How did God create? With words. "And God *said* . . . " We create the same way—with words. We speak both actions and things into existence by saying, "I am going," "I am doing," "I will be . . . "

God has said that "death and life are in the power of the tongue" (Prov. 18:21). We receive Jesus (Life) by speaking words of faith and believing. We hurt, kill, heal, or bless with our words. "There is one who speaks like the piercings of a sword: But the tongue of the wise promotes health" (Prov. 12:18).

I realize that the magnitude of the subject of communication cannot be adequately handled in a single chapter, or in a single book for that matter. My purpose in presently addressing the subject is this: The apostle Paul admonished us all (and I believe this as a personal dictum), "Be diligent to present yourself approved to God, a worker . . ." (2 Tim. 2:15). As a worker appointed to the position of administrator in the Body of Christ by godly men, it is my responsibility to function in the most effective way possible. And if I am to be the effective worker that God desires—and that I myself desire to be—I must learn to communicate effectively. God has given me the ability. It is now up to me to put it to work.

CHAPTER 9

Learn to Be
an Enthusiast

Learn to get excited about your work. There is no position that can make an enthused administrator of you, but an enthused administrator who can get excited about his work can turn any mundane job into an elevated position. You can say with Paul, "I magnify my ministry . . . " (Rom. 11:13).

People often say to me, "If I only had a glamorous position like yours, with all that world travel, then I could get excited about my work." Or, "If you knew how difficult my job is, you wouldn't tell me to get excited about it."

Work—wherever you find it—implies the same thing: detailed monotony, preparation, striving, and weariness. Life is so daily, isn't it? But that's what we all have to overcome, no matter what our work is. It's easier to get excited about something I'm *not* doing or what someone else may be doing.

In spite of the fact that I thoroughly enjoy my work, I sometimes think how green the grass may be in the other person's yard—the person who doesn't have to travel excessively, raise funds, and be weighted down with "administrivia." But those times don't last long! I readily come back to a deep understanding and appreciation that I am in the place of God's choosing. Doing His will is all that really matters for any of us.

But if I have to do it, and have to learn and grow and plan and persevere, then it's *work*—and work isn't fun, no matter where you do it.

But to learn the art of truly being a Christian administrator, I must learn to get enthused about *my* work. Not someone else's, not the work I'm going to do someday, but my work now. A bonus to think of is this: if you learn to get excited about your job on those ordinary days, think how tremendous it will be on the special days. There is nothing that can make you more excited about your work than a sense of its importance. Only you can give your job dignity.

If you don't have a realization of the importance of your work, ask God to give it to you. Believe that He will as you begin to act accordingly. Believe your job is worth doing and your belief will help you create the reality. There is no other way to learn to be an enthusiastic person without being totally involved and committed to whatever you are engaged in.

Futhermore, learn to be thankful for your job. At this writing, nearly 11 percent of our national work force is unemployed. According to the first chapter of Romans, one of the early signals of apostasy is refusing to worship God and give Him thanks. Even if you dislike your work or would prefer another job, take a moment to thank the Lord you *have* a job!

The Administrative Attitude

A job as a Christian administrator is something God calls you to, and God says that you are to "walk worthy of the calling with which you were called" (Eph. 4:1). The things Jesus did were of the most commonplace nature, and this is an indication to me that it takes all of God's power in me to do the most commonplace things in His way. That means learning to do everything with all your heart. Enthusiasm is an attitude.

There are few, if any, jobs in which ability alone is sufficient.

Attitudes play a vitally important role. What do you think about other people? About the people you work with? Your attitude toward other people is terribly important, because it affects—sometimes determines—the way they feel about you. It has a lot to do with your enthusiasm toward your job and life in general. But even more importantly, your attitude toward others tells them about your relationship to God.

Terry, the son of one of my colleagues, went to South America one summer with his friend Phil on a missionary-aid program. The boys were in the village one market day; it was bustling with people, animals, and confusion. They saw a small girl standing somewhat apart from the crowd with a basket of fruit for sale. As they watched, the girl was roughly jostled; and her fruit went rolling in the dust in every direction. Instead of helping her, the men who had jostled the girl shouted as they ran off, "Move out of the way." She began to pick up her fruit, trying to wipe them clean on her dirty dress.

Phil saw her dilemma and moved quickly to help her. As he knelt beside her in the dirt, picking up and carefully wiping the fruit, then placing it back in her basket, she stared at him through tear-filled eyes. When he looked back at her she asked, "Say, mister, are you Jesus?"

Phil said his life was dramatically changed with the realization that other people may be basing their idea of Jesus Christ on his behavior. Phil's spontaneous, outgoing act resulted in an enthusiastic response from a girl quite unused to having someone reach out in love and caring.

Cultivating Enthusiasm

It is true that some people are naturally more outgoing and gregarious than others. I can hear someone saying, "I can't be very enthusiastic because I'm an introvert." My response is, "Be an enthusiastic introvert!" Enthusiasm and maintaining a high noise level are in no way synonymous. For those to whom enthusiasm does not come naturally, it can be cultivated.

The word "enthusiasm" comes from the Greek words *en theos*, which mean "in God." If you have accepted Jesus Christ as your Savior, then you are "in God." And when you know who you are in God, you can't help but get excited. At first, you must consciously put your eyes, your voice, your spirit—in other words, yourself—into your appreciation of people. But you will be surprised at how quickly it becomes second nature.

One way to begin cultivating enthusiasm is by learning to say something positive to others. But you say, "That is impossible. You don't know my boss." Or, "Obviously you've never worked with a group like my group." Learning to say something positive is a journey, a process. For many people, most of their conversation is negative. Some people can't wait to expose negative nugget after negative nugget for all to hear. I'm talking about downright pessimism. God speaks of that attitude when He says, "The wicked is ensnared by the transgression of his lips" (Prov. 12:13).

I am convinced there is nothing that will improve the atmosphere and productivity of an organization, home, or church like an enthusiastic person who genuinely affirms others. I believe it is possible to say something positive to almost everybody—if we really want to. But the problem with many of us is we don't want to make the effort to do it.

Attitudes are often more important than facts. When discussing a negative attitude with employees, I have heard people say, "I can't help how I feel." That's not exactly true. How you feel is created in part by what you think, and God says you can control your thoughts. As a matter of fact, He has commanded us to "cast down arguments and every high thing that exalts itself against the knowledge of God, [and bring] every thought into captivity to the obedience of Christ" (2 Cor. 10:5).

Even though we try to filter out undesirable thoughts, it seems we sometimes cannot. At such times, we may accept negative attitudes which flood us with fear, hopelessness, inferiority, or hate. If we remain passive and allow this to happen, we will continuously nurture our feelings—resentment, self-condemnation, anxiety, or depression—mulling over the thoughts that stimulate them instead of casting them out.

Poor administrators pour out their own negative thoughts and feelings upon anyone within hearing. The result is that negative emotions and attitudes continue to multiply. Distressing and depressing emotions do not just happen. They do not just float in from something outside of us and descend upon us against our will. They arise from our thoughts. The only thing that keeps our undesirable emotions and attitudes alive are our own negative thought patterns that we *choose to accept*.

This is why God insists on His children having disciplined minds, and why He repeatedly warns us of the danger of entertaining evil and destructive thoughts (anything contrary to God's Word). Such thoughts are extremely dangerous—to both our souls and our bodies.

There is a growing number of medical doctors who now believe that most illness and disease are caused by stress-producing fear. Satan knows this to be true. This is the reason he is so subtle in dropping suggestions and insinuations of fear into our minds.

God knows that the fear of external things, be they problems or people, can literally kill us. He has told us nearly four hundred times in His Word to "fear not." God desires to protect and strengthen us with His Word, which is why He tells us to "be transformed (changed) by the [entire] renewal of your mind—by its new ideals and its new attitude—so that you may prove [for yourselves] what is the good and acceptable and perfect will of God" (Rom. 12:2, *Amplified Bible*).

When we continually practice renewing our minds with the Word of God, we protect ourselves against negative thoughts, thus negative attitudes, because we will then start thinking like God thinks. And those Godlike thoughts will produce Godlike attitudes that promote a healthy, Godlike atmosphere.

In 2 Corinthians 7:6–7 Paul speaks about the positive atmosphere created by Titus's presence: "Then God who cheers those who are discouraged refreshed us by the arrival of Titus. Not only was his presence a joy, but also the news that he brought of the wonderful time he had with you" (TLB). I think every administrator should ask himself the question, "Does my *presence* refresh those who may be discouraged?"

Another trait to develop is that of seeing positive solutions in every situation. Make every problem a challenge. Back when the late Edward Cole was president of General Motors he was asked, "What makes you different from other men—why have you succeeded over thousands of others to the top job at G.M.?" He thought for a moment and replied, "I love problems!"

Do you notice how quickly some people jump to negative conclusions about things they see and hear? Suppose someone called you to the phone and announced, "It's your boss!" Would your first thought be, "Tremendous, he wants to commend me on last week's project"? Or would it be, "Now what did I do?"

Learn to be a positive realist. Develop your creative ability to recognize and find answers. Sam Moore, president of Thomas Nelson Publishers, has a sign on his office door, "Bring me your solutions, not your problems." Quit speaking the problem and start speaking the solution, be it to your subordinates or to your superior.

Have you noticed that Jesus rarely addressed the problem? Instead He nearly always spoke of the solution. And He told us to do the same thing.

For assuredly, I say to you, whoever says to this mountain, "Be removed and be cast into the sea," and does not doubt in his heart, but believes that those things he says will come to pass, he will have whatever he says (Mark 11:23).

God's Word tells us that we will have what we say. "For by your words you will be justified, and by your words you will be condemned" (Matt. 12:37). "A man will be satisfied with good by the fruit of his mouth" (Prov. 12:14). "A man has joy by the answer of his mouth, and a word spoken in due season, how good it is!" (Prov. 15:23).

Learn to be a "benedictor!" The close of a Christian liturgy of worship is called the benediction. It comes from the Latin *bene* (good) and *dictum* (word)—the good word! A benediction is God's parting good word to us as we move back out into the world. Begin speaking good words at your job and around your home. If you do, you will find yourself living in a better world, a more enthusiastic world. For your enthusiastic words will be reflected back to you from the people to whom you give them. Words are tremendous multipliers!

In the last chapter I mentioned the emotional impact of the message and how many psychologists believe the largest part of this impact comes from body language, which includes facial expressions. Our facial expressions are trainable. I want to encourage you to consciously begin to train yours to reflect an attitude of enthusiasm. Let your light shine. Begin with the thoughts that prompt pleasant expressions, and deliberately practice those expressions. The more you practice, the more spontaneous they become. Just as you taught the muscles of your hand to hold a pen and form letters in early grade school, so you can also teach the muscles in your face to express your feelings attractively in your administrative post.

Put a smile in your voice! A smile can be heard as well as seen. One of my secretaries used to keep a mirror by her phone to remind her to smile before speaking into the phone. A person will age himself quickly when he no longer wears a happy, interested, "in God," alive expression. The spark, the radiance that Jesus gives comes from the inside, but is best expressed through your physical characteristics.

Enthusiasm Brings Encouragement

Inherent in the art of being a Christian administrator is the ability to be an encourager. In order to be an encourager to others you must like and enjoy people, and in order to like people you must first like yourself.

Sometimes people say, "I don't even like the way I look. How can I like myself?" Our rejection of ourselves is usually a response to the value that other people place on our appearance, abilities, social skills, or social background. However, the true basis for self-acceptance is a clear understanding and acceptance of the values and purposes that God has for us.

God created you. "Try to realize what this means—the Lord is God! He made us—we are his people, the sheep of his pasture" (Ps. 100:3 TLB).

Woe to the man who fights with his Creator. Does the pot argue with its maker? Does the clay dispute with him who forms it, saying, "Stop, you're doing it wrong!" or the pot exclaim, "How clumsy can you be!"? Woe to the baby just being born who squalls to his father and mother, "Why have you produced me? Can't you do anything right at all?" Jehovah, the Holy One of Israel, Israel's Creator, says: What right have you to question what I do? Who are you to command me concerning the work of my hands? (Is. 45:9–11 TLB).

If you have any doubt about God designing you just the way you are with your own personal gifts, read Psalm 139. Read it in several versions and let the love and care of God saturate your life.

God does not want you to compare yourself with others. Most of us have probably used the expression "that's like comparing apples and oranges," meaning a comparison cannot be made because of unique differences. And administrators can make some unwise decisions by trying to make comparisons in distinctly different situations. God says we also behave unwisely when we try to compare ourselves with others. "However, when they measure themselves with themselves and compare themselves with one another, they are without understanding and behave unwisely" (2 Cor. 10:12 *Amplified Bible*).

God made you for a specific reason. The fear of other people's judgment will make us sterile and prevent us from being fruitful. Remember the parable of the master who gave talents to his servants. All except one used them and increased them. But that one servant hid his talent in the earth instead of putting it to use. When the master asked him why, he said, "I was afraid" (Matt. 25:25). But God says He "has not given us a spirit of fear, but of power and of love and of a sound mind" (1 Tim. 1:7).

How many times have we neglected to move out in God's power and strength to develop the opportunities He has given us, allowing the fear of failure to keep us from becoming all that God has planned for us to be? Remember:

We are God's [own] handiwork (His workmanship), recreated in Christ Jesus, [born anew] that we may do those good works which God predestined (planned beforehand) for us, (taking paths which He prepared ahead of time) that we should walk in them—living the good life which He prearranged and made ready for us to live (Eph. 2:10 *Amplified Bible*).

My appearance can be altered by God's Word. When God's Word becomes the core of a person's thought life, there is a glow about the person that attracts others.

And all of us, as with unveiled face, [because we] continued to behold [in the word of God] as in a mirror the glory of the Lord, are constantly being transfigured into His very own image in ever increasing splendor and from one degree of glory to another; [for this comes] from the Lord [Who is] the Spirit (2 Cor. 3:18 *Amplified Bible*).

After many years, I can still recall the glow on the face of the sixteen-year-old prostitute in Bristol, England, who came to faith in Christ late at night on the streets as a result of the witness of some of my Youth for Christ colleagues. She immediately began coming to the sessions of the Youth Congress being held, and rarely have any of us seen such a transformation of a person's appearance—from the "mod" look of young people in Britain in those days to the modest look of one who has surrendered to Christ. Over the years she has grown in grace and has served the Lord. It was, for her, a life-transforming experience in which her dress, her looks, her behavior all drastically and dramatically changed overnight. This is what happens when God moves into a life. In this particular situation, it was one of the most dramatic and unforgettable experiences that I have known.

God never stops helping me improve myself. You will never come to the place where you can truly say, "I will never be anything more than I am." I have seen so many administrators curtail their potential because they developed a preconceived idea of their limitations. Remember that predestined growth by a person in any area—whether physical, intellectual, or spiritual—limits and ultimately cripples.

A familiar illustration of this is to be seen in the way young Chinese girls years ago had their feet bound. The purpose was to limit their growth so they would develop petite feet and have a hobbling walk that was considered attractive. It was a crippling and painful custom.

If we refuse to take time to expose ourselves to the unlimited gifts of God and don't work to make the most of the attributes and opportunities He gives us, then we are just as surely "binding" our lives. As a result our professional and personal growth will be stunted. Speaking of this very principle, the apostle Paul said:

> And I am convinced and sure of this very thing, that He Who began a good work in you will continue until the day of Jesus Christ—right up to the time of His return—developing [that good work] and perfecting and bringing it to full completion in you (Phil. 1:6 *Amplified Bible*).

God expects me to help others.

> What a wonderful God we have—he is the Father of our Lord Jesus Christ, the source of every mercy, and the one who so wonderfully comforts and strengthens us in our hardships and trials. And why does he do this? So that when others are troubled, needing our sympathy and encouragement, we can pass on to them this same help and comfort God has given us (2 Cor. 1:3–4 TLB).

All of us know of individuals who have the very special gift of helps. My wife, Dorothy, has exercised this gift so often as she has stood by neighbors—and strangers—whom, in an uncanny way, she has recognized as needing a word of encouragement and help.

We in administrative leadership need to look for opportunities to minister to hurting people with whom we work. But we often get so engrossed in our work that we don't take the time to encourage or help the ones close by who may be struggling. Unfortunately, we probably don't notice them—and never will unless we make it a part of our ministry to look for ways to exercise the gift of helps.

As you share yourself with others, it helps to meet their

needs. Through helping them, you will realize that you have been of worth to them and are fulfilling a part of God's purpose for your life.

Help others develop a sense of self-worth. Learn to express appreciation and approval. Praise others frequently for a job well done. And mean it! Henrietta Mears, founder of Gospel Light Publishing Company, used to say, "Every time I meet someone, I visualize a sign across their chest which says, 'My name is _____ , please help me feel important.' " The words you use in expressing praise are very important. Be specific about achievement, not general about character.

In your administrative responsibilities, look for special activities and accomplishments in which you can affirm associates and employees. Genuine "strokes," or compliments, are so appreciated and will help assure further quality work. Everyone is grateful for special expressions of appreciation. A simple note, a word of praise, a compliment in the presence of others mean much more than we often realize—and it costs nothing!

You may be a natural "appreciator-in-depth." If you are not, I promise that if you will begin to seek out specific things to admire in others, you will not only find that your appreciation is received with great pleasure, but you will also get enjoyment yourself from your new attitude. After all, if we appreciate something, it is usually for a specific reason. If we train ourselves to analyze the reason, we have the basis for appreciation in depth.

Gideon was an administrator who showed great wisdom in this regard. In Judges, chapter 8, verses 1–3, we see him lifting up the feats of others above his own; and by so doing he prevented strife and gave encouragement.

> Now the men of Ephraim said to [Gideon], "Why have you done this to us by not calling us when you went to fight with the Midianites?" And they reprimanded him sharply. So he said to

them, "What have I done now in comparison with you? Is not the gleaning of the grapes of Ephraim better than the vintage of Abiezer? God has delivered into your hands the princes of Midian, Oreb and Zeeb. And what was I able to do in comparison with you?" Then their anger toward him abated when he said that.

Your attitude toward those around you can increase their own self-esteem. Never depreciate another person; learn never to say less about a person than what God says. This does not mean that you cannot point out error and shortcomings; but it does mean that when criticism becomes necessary, it should always be constructive.

Prior to offering criticism, look for something for which you can compliment the individual. If the person you need to criticize knows that you have his best interest at heart, the criticism is much more palatable. Constructive criticism is an important element for all of us as we grow in our work responsibilities and in life itself. This is true with employees and associates, as well as with our children. We should make it known throughout the organization that we have need of constructive criticism as a means of growth and development. Let others know that we need and expect this from them.

Criticism should always leave the person feeling he has been helped. Goethe said, "If you treat a man as he is, he will stay as he is. But if you treat him as if he were what he ought to be, and could be, he will become that bigger and better man." So begin to express appreciation to your colleagues for what they are and encourage them in all that they are capable of becoming. Concentrate on strengths and virtues, instead of weaknesses and faults. Expect the best in others—it's a self-fulfilling prophecy!

Thinking Creatively

Some weeks ago a friend of mine was taking his small daughter on a cruise to California's Catalina Island. It was one of our beautiful, clear southern California days. Suddenly the little girl exclaimed, "Daddy, I can look farther than my eyes can see!"

Think about that. "I can look farther than my eyes can see!" What a wonderfully perceptive child.

Creative Imagination

Too few administrators possess the ability to look any further than their eyes can see. We might have had it once, as that child still does; but for too many administrators it has been stifled. Stifled in the petty routines of a regimented network of papers and projects and in the prejudices that develop in an organizational world. Yet if we are to be creative administrators—and effective innovators—we must release that dormant ability. We must again learn to look beyond the horizon.

Perhaps even more importantly, we must *want* to look beyond the horizon. For a great majority of administrators this is not easy, and for some it is exceptionally difficult. Most administrators desperately seek an order and pattern to life—one that will leave them with a feeling of constancy, not change. Consequently, they are not receptive to rearrangements. But our imagination should be one of our most cherished faculties, for it will enable every administrator to realize that God "is able to do exceedingly abundantly above all that we ask or think" (Eph. 3:20).

The imagination of our colleagues should also be cherished, for it follows that in any organization the administrator can never be the sole source of innovation, no matter how great his genius. How, then, can he draw from his colleagues the wealth of their creative thinking except by stimulating their imaginations?

Creative imagination is that part of the mind which generates desires, thoughts, hopes, and dreams. Everything that has ever been achieved started first as an unseen spark in a creative imagination. "In the beginning God created . . . " God spoke into existence His imaginings. He created man in His own image and gave to mankind the gift of imagination so that we can also form, hold, and achieve images.

Then when Jesus came, He liberated man's imagination by telling him, "I assure you that the man who believes in Me will do the same things that I have done, yes, and he will do even greater things than these" (John 14:12 *Phillips*). As an administrator, you may inhibit the growth of your employee's imagination unless you dare to believe that what Jesus said is true.

The part of your mind that plays the greatest role in achievement is that part of your mind that imagines. We spend years developing the part of our mind that reasons, memorizes, and learns; but almost no time is given to developing the immense potential of our imagination. Yet the untapped power of our imagination is unlimited.

God created man's brain in two distinct parts, each having different functions. The left side of the brain is basically concerned with logic and speech—it thinks. The right side of the brain is related to intuition and creativity—it knows. It is visual in orientation. It is the right side of the brain that some of us tend to neglect.

An interesting experiment was done at Stanford University by Robert McKim, Professor of Design Engineering. He created what he calls an "imaginarium," for the purpose of tapping the vast unknown riches of the mind's eye, because he was concerned about finding ways to expand his students' thinking about design problems. McKim's experiments led him to design his own version of a geodesic dome, which serves as a special environment where people can get away from noise and other distractions. "The person who learns to use his imagination flexibly," McKim explained, "sees creatively."

And this "seeing creatively" is a rich source of ideas and mental pictures that can be developed. A person's imagination reflects an ability to visualize something that has been neither seen nor experienced before. The creative act thrives in an environment of mutual stimulation, feedback, and constructive criticism—in a "community of creativity."

Administering Creativity

Every administrator must help provide a creative environment which will make certain that new ideas are brought forward, evaluated, and carried through. We must instill in our people the knowledge that we not only recognize the necessity of new ideas and experimentation, but that we actively encourage the unconventional solution to the conventional problem.

Now I know as well as the next person that the individual who attempts the new, the different, the one who seeks innovation is likely to make some mistakes. But, isn't it infinitely more desirable to assure a man of some reasonable measure of freedom in order to spark some fresh, imaginative thinking than to slap him down when he commits his first error—and perhaps stifle him forever?

Sometimes we forget how eager we were to try out our new ideas. All our people, I'm sure, have new ideas, too. They're itching to take a crack at putting them into practice, to swim in a little deeper water and justify their membership on the team. Good. Give them the opportunity. They may come up with some harebrained ideas, some of them simply not workable. But when they do, don't dampen their creative ardor by telling them that they have made a mistake. Instead, advise them tactfully to try again and this time to use a little different approach.

Administrators can help produce ideas by a conscious creative effort, and in this process, it pays to focus our aim. We should first make our target as clear as possible.

Creativity and Research

The process of research is to pull the problem apart into its separate components, a great many of which you already know about. When you get it pulled apart, you can work on the things you don't know. The importance of problem definition was stressed by Albert Einstein in these words: "The formulation of a problem is often far more essential than its solution, which may be merely a matter of mathematical or experimental skill."

Let me give you an illustration of how consciously searching for a solution to a problem can spell out opportunity. A few years ago manufacturers were unable to give consumers as good a fit in shirts as in collars. The trouble was that collars had always been washed after being made, while if shirts were washed that way, they would lose some of their fine finish—would look as though they were not new. So, on his own initiative, Sanford Cluett decided to find a way to shrink cloth without putting it in water.

At the cotton mills Mr. Cluett saw that in the finishing process the cloth was always pulled through the various processes of bleaching and mercerization. In fact, the cloth was sewed together into strips as long as fourteen miles and then pulled through the mill. This naturally distorted the fabric. He discovered that if this distortion was taken out, most of the shrinkage would be eliminated. So he built a machine which automatically restored the cloth to equilibrium—in other words, pushed the stretch back. Although the "Sanforized" process was designed for cotton goods only, its success has led to other related creations, thus typifying how we can reach out for targets by grasping problems, and how one target can create another.

When my former World Vision colleague, Bobb Biehl, was seeking to find ways of helping us raise funds for our World Hunger program, he began an experiment with various means of involving entire families in this ministry. He had no thought of anything apart from a direct mail presentation; but as he worked away at his drawing board, he began to think of the primacy the Word of God gives to bread and the emphasis of our Lord on His being the Bread of Life.

The thought struck Bobb that a small loaf of bread symbolized both spiritual and physical life. From this concept came his idea of the "Love Loaves" (little banks shaped like loaves of bread), which have been the means of raising literally millions of dollars for world hunger needs. This serendipitous idea became an integral part of our world famine program.

Creative triumphs have also come from experiments done for the sole purpose of satisfying intellectual curiosity. Michael Faraday went at it blindly when, in 1831, he discovered how electricity could be produced. He had no target. He merely wondered what would happen if he mounted a copper disc between two poles of a horseshoe magnet and made it spin. To his amazement, it produced electric current.

Creative Questioning

Now and then someone asks a question which leads to an especially productive answer. One example of this was reported by the Department of Agriculture a number of years ago. Baby pigs are often crushed by their mothers rolling over upon them. An unknown "thinker-upper" asked whether pig mortality in a farrowing house could not be remedied by simply tilting the floor. This led to a system which is now working well. Since mamma pigs like to lie down with their backs uphill and piglets like to travel downhill, the tilted floor tends to keep the baby from under the recumbent mother. Now no more crushed pigs!

I remember the day Bob Pierce called me from Asia during the early days of the Vietnam conflict. He was deeply concerned about the lack of material help for wounded Vietnam War veterans when they were brought into the poorly equipped military hospitals. "What can we do to help them?" he asked. "Think about it," he said, "and let's investigate it when I get home."

From that question came the famous World Vision "Viet Kit" program, with millions of these kits being prepared by church groups, schools, youth societies, and families. Other kits were distributed to Vietnamese children, soldiers, and widows. Bob's question led to redemptive answers.

Questions have long been recognized as a way to stimulate imagination. Professors who have sought to make their teaching more creative have often employed this device. In practical problem-solving we can give conscious guidance to our thinking by asking ourselves questions.

Creative Readjustment of Objectives

Administrators also should recognize that innovative aims often change. This is not an unexpected turn of affairs in

organized creativity, for problem-solving often calls for refor-
mulating the problem itself and then solving the new problem.
It pays to assess our aims and objectives. Countless people have
spent endless hours and enormous amounts of creative energy
on projects of no useful purpose.

I, too, have at times set forth in search of will-o'-the-wisps. I
recall during my Youth-for-Christ days dreaming largely of a
great international Christian youth conference to be held in
Jerusalem. We made extensive plans, visited possible sites, spent
months in developing plans—only to finally find that the
logistics, language barrier, political problems, and finances
were all beyond our reach. Much energy and time were expended in the project, which undoubtedly could have been better
invested in other programs.

It was a valuable lesson for many of us. I realize that had I
analyzed those limitations earlier, I could have invested those
creative hours in something of greater promise. Through the
years I have found that there are many ways of learning to use
creative time in a productive manner.

Alex Morrison, famous golf instructor and author of *Better
Golf Without Practice,* instructs his readers to use creative time
in a productive manner. He enables golfers to eliminate strokes
from their scores simply through mental practice. Morrison
demonstrates the correct swing and gives a few pointers in the
area of golf. Then he asks the student to spend at least five
minutes each day relaxed in an easy chair, eyes closed, picturing
himself on the golf course playing the game perfectly.

"You must," says Morrison, "have a clear mental picture of
the correct thing before you can do it successfully. That can be
acquired through instruction, by watching championship golf,
or studying action pictures of golfers you admire." (Incidental-
ly, my problem is that I don't take the necessary five or ten
minutes!)

One reason mental practice so often brings prompt improvement is that for the first time, instead of struggling to remember many isolated ideas, you can form a complete pattern. This is why books showing you how to do tasks correctly are so important. The more you study the illustration and picture it in your mind's eye, the more proficient you will become at this and the more quickly difficult tasks are made easier.

Inhibitors to Creativity

Most administrators know creative thinking or innovation when they see it. However, it is quite another thing to identify those things which stifle creative thinking, and to root them out. Let me point out a few of the inhibitors I see to genuine creative thought.

First, in our society there seems to be a cultural distaste for innovation. Years ago we admired and rewarded innovation and creativity. Today, however, innovation frequently goes unrewarded. Society is fearful, and so it resents those who might tip the canoe. Security has become the slogan of the secular society.

But in the light of the Christian's resources, fear and fearfulness are self-defeating. Besides, they do not come from God, who, instead of fear, has given us the spirit "of power and of love and of a sound mind" (2 Tim. 1:7). Therefore, the person who is rooted in God need never be fearful of exercising his God-given creativity.

Second, within the organization itself there may be a tendency to hold the power of all decision-making at the top. This is based on the mistaken notion that the only competent, intelligent individuals are those at the top. Some of the most creative ideas can come from the ranks.

I mentioned earlier the popular Love Loaves which Bobb Biehl developed for World Vision; this program continues on to this day. In addition, we have a thirty-hour famine program for young people that teaches them to identify with world hunger needs. This entire successful ministry has been conceived and developed by some of our beautiful middle-management people.

A third barrier to innovation centers in the individual himself. We generally live far below our creative limits. Scientific tests for aptitudes have revealed the relative universality of creative potential. An analysis of almost all the psychological tests ever made points to the conclusion that creative talent is fairly evenly distributed, and that our creative efficiency varies more in ratio to our output of mental energy than to our inborn talent. This would have to be so because the Bible states that we are created to be like God.

As God concluded His creative process in Genesis, He said, " 'Let Us make man in Our image, according to Our likeness.'...So God created man in His own image" (Gen. 1:26-27). The Hebrew word used here is *demuth*, which denotes likeness in every way. Hence, since God is a creative being, it follows that man is *by nature* also a creative being.

When one fully realizes the creative potential God has given him, he can rejoice. Jesus said, "If you live in Me—abide vitally united to Me—and My words remain in you and continue to live in your hearts, ask whatever you will and it shall be done for you" (John 15:7 *Amplified Bible*).

So to the degree that His words live in us, we actually have or possess His mind (see 1 Cor. 2:16) and, consequently, His creativity. Thus the creative Godlikeness, the *demuth* of Genesis 1:27, becomes ours on a practical level; and we can ask for and receive creative assistance from our Father.

The barriers, therefore, to innovation and creativity lie primarily in these three areas: within our society, within organizations, within individuals. If we are to encourage our creative forces, we must be aware of these inhibitors and substitute a climate that facilitates innovation and growth.

An Atmosphere for Growth

One thing administrators can do is provide an atmosphere in which the individual's sensitivity can flourish rather than wither away. Innovation comes from awareness of a need or a problem. The problem may exist within the individual himself, or it may be present in the organization or in the public it serves. To solve it requires an openness of mind—a capacity for being receptive to new ideas.

We must also enlarge a man's knowledge about what is going on around him and encourage him to learn more about his own field. We can give him the opportunity to develop and improve the techniques and skills of his area of work.

It is important that every person should master the fundamentals of the job; for while the novice may generate insight and creative ideas on his own, he usually is in no position to use it to the organization's advantage. The novice may not possess the skills and techniques required to follow through on ideas. This is important because, for an idea to be a good one, it must be carried through to its ultimate conclusions. Otherwise it is a passing fancy—a wish, a dream. It must be communicated, it must be implemented, it must be put into effect. Some people can come up with great ideas, but they cannot implement them. They are "idea men" and either cannot or will not carry them through to completion. However, we need these people. In baseball it's pretty hard to bench a .400 hitter who can't field.

We must then develop these idea people's ability to implement, or put others alongside them who have ability in this field. In short, we need to create teams capable of supplementing thoughts with action. We must also provide enough time for the innovator to create. He needs time for preparation, time for the incubation of ideas, time for evaluation and redefinition, and time for complete double-checking and follow-up.

As administrators provide this "community of creativity,"

the interaction it stimulates will serve as a catalyst to others. And in this community there must be free exchange of ideas, constructive criticism, and disagreement without penalty. In addition, we must give the innovator a sense of belonging to management. For only if he participates in the formulation of goals, and only if he is part of the broad creative effort of the entire organization, can his contributions be real. And don't forget, people support what they help create.

We must recognize the *demuth*, the Godlikeness, of every person at every level in every type of work. We need to remember that each man has within himself the potential for innovation, no matter how little formal education he may have had, no matter how humble his background. We must use every resource of every individual, for the sake of that person, for the sake of the organization, and most importantly for the sake of God's kingdom. We must be careful that we do not put people in strait jackets—that we do not try to make them over in our own image and likeness, causing them to become only a distorted caricature.

Make no mistake about it—a most important job for all administrators is to bring into existence an innovative organization. How well each one of us does this will determine the productive future growth of our organization. A creative organization comes only to those administrators who are intensely committed—first to God and to His call upon their lives—and then to a burning desire to help bring about conditions that will stimulate the natural growth of creativity in other individuals.

CHAPTER 11

Without a Vision
Even the Administrator Perishes!

The source of this chapter title is obvious, coming as it does from Proverbs 29:18; "Where there is no vision, the people perish" (KJV).

A proverb is a truism. It speaks of a true principle, something which is true for any people, in any age, in any land. The words of Solomon are as true for me as they were when he wrote them. They are as true for God's people today as they were the first day God revealed them.

To me, they are very practical and can be applied to business. The word "vision" in this context speaks to me of the concept of what's happening now, and ideas, plans, and projections for tomorrow. For the future.

The Crucial Place of Vision

Placed in that context, one can easily see that (to paraphrase) "where there are no plans or goals, the people drift into a meaningless, pointless existence." If I am living merely for today, with no thought of the future, the days will pass one by one, followed by the months and years in swift succession, until old age and death.

Such a life seems to me to be meaningless. The song that was so popular twenty years ago was an outgrowth of such an existence. "Qué será, será," it went. "What will be, will be." Some of the words are so self-defeating. "What will be, will be. The future's not mine to see. Qué será, será." Apparently a whole generation of youth picked up on it. They sang it, talked it, joked about it, believed it.

I believe that attitude was and is a deadly ruse of Satan.

There is a degree of the future which we cannot see. That is true. But, on the other hand, it is also true that God has given me the ability to *plan my future*. If I use my God-given intelligence, I can think. I can think ahead. I can then think of ways and means to achieve that which I have thought. And by so doing, I take the responsibility for my own future.

As an individual, I have the responsibility of stewardship for all that God has given me—my life, my family, my potential. If I squander them away either by dissipation or disregard, I can hardly expect God's approving words, "Well done, good and faithful servant" (Matt. 25:21).

Therefore, I choose to seek the visions, the plans, the revelations of God's opportunities. Dr. Paul Yonggi Cho, pastor of the largest church in the world in Seoul, South Korea, believes in visions. I have been to his church, and I have seen the result of his dreams and visions. Starting from nothing, as Pastor Cho did, one can only gasp at the immensity of the physical dimensions of the present church structure. As of this writing, the membership is rapidly approaching the 300,000 mark.

How did it all happen?

Dr. Cho described it this way in a recent address to students at the Rhema Bible School in Broken Arrow, Oklahoma: "Dreams and visions are the language of the Holy Spirit. God speaks to us in our spirits, by His Spirit. When we learn how to approach Him, and ask Him to do so, that's how He guides us. . . ."

As a young Bible school student, Cho conceived the dream

of building the biggest church in the world. But the realization of the dream didn't come overnight. By successive states, Cho says, "I became *pregnant with my vision*." That is, he planted the seed in his mind. He continues:

> Then I nurtured the vision. It grew within me. Just as the embryonic fetus grows within the womb of a pregnant woman, that "fetus" vision grew within me. Then I nurtured it. I fed it. I thought about that "baby" that was to be "born." I made plans and preparations for it. And like that pregnant woman, I became large and heavy with the vision. . . .

When the day for the birthing of the vision came, Cho was ready for it, and the church was born. Then, like the infant grows, so grew the church. It is still growing. And it will continue to grow, for Cho continually feeds it, nurtures it, *expects and plans for it to grow*.

The Work of Being Visionary

We have sought to use the same process at World Vision.

My colleagues and I ask God for creative ideas, plans, and goals. We work on them—pray over them! We meditate on His Word. We try to heed the advice of Proverbs 16:3. "Commit your works to the LORD, and your thoughts will be established". Or as the *Amplified Version* reads, "commit and trust them wholly to Him; [He will cause your thoughts to become agreeable to His will, and] so shall your *plans* be established and succeed."

At this point meditation (thinking God's thoughts after Him) is so important. Where does this happen? In my mind, of course. That's where my thoughts are. And God said He would cause my *thoughts* to become agreeable (or to come in line with) His will. When that happens, I cannot help but succeed.

148

Because that means that God's plans and my plans have become one.

Another Scripture that has challenged and drawn me is Joshua 1:8. "This Book of the Law," it reads, "shall not depart from your mouth, but you shall meditate in it day and night." Meditate. What does that mean? To me it means I'm to roll those words of God's around *in my mind*, day and night. I'm to think about them, delight in them (see Ps. 1:2), act on them.

When I do that, the results are dramatic.

The rest of the verse reads, "that you may observe to do according to all that is written in it. [That's it, *acting* on the Word of God.] For then you will make your way prosperous, and then you will have good success."

That's God's desire for every administrator—success.

In my business career, I have made it the rule of my life to get away from the office for certain specified times just to meditate and pray. I do this often and it pays rich rewards. At least twice a year I engage a room at a hotel, where I go alone for two days of prayer and seeking the Lord. I take only my Bible. I cannot be reached while I am there. These are precious days with the Lord. I seek to listen to Him, talk to Him, worship Him, receive from Him.

And it's during these days that often a special word from the Lord has come to my heart that, hopefully, has affected the future of World Vision.

I write down the concepts He has given me. I meditate on them. I plan them, project them, make preparations for their advent. And they come into reality. Why? Because God promised (in Joshua 1:8) that if I do so, I will prosper—and *everything I do will prosper* (see Ps. 1:3).

Warning: Don't Overdo a Vision

I have an aversion to many of the so-called "prosperity"

concepts that have been promulgated during this past decade. Some of them seem to promise automatic financial rewards from God, just for the asking. I know of some who have even gone to the extreme of quitting their jobs and trusting God to supply all their needs.

In my judgment, God just doesn't work that way. At least if He does, I have not found it to be His modus operandi for me!

Without getting too theological, let me share with you some Scriptural truths in this regard. There are quite a number of Hebrew and Greek words that carry with them the connotation of success and prosperity. I'm not going to give an exegesis of these words, but I am going to summarize some of the results I've come up with. For those who are interested in doing so, I recommend they investigate *Strong's Exhaustive Concordance* and *Thayer's Greek-English Lexicon of the New Testament*.

One of the words of great interest is the Hebrew word rendered "prosper and have good success" in Joshua 1:8, which I have already quoted. It actually means "be caused to go on prosperously." I like that. But what, exactly, does prosper mean? I checked that out, in both the Hebrew and Greek, and arrived at some very interesting conclusions.

The following is a list of how these words are rendered in English:

- come to maturity
- deal wisely
- be in good health
- grow stronger, advance, get bigger
- move ahead, go forward
- be holy, be clean, be acceptable
- go on prosperously
- cause to go on prosperously

So you can see, as I did, that the acceptance of Jesus as Savior and Lord does not *automatically* guarantee financial prosperity. But seeking "first the kingdom of God," as Jesus advocated in Matthew 6:33, will put us into right relationship with both Jesus and His Father. That, of course, is the beginning of success.

I believe it is axiomatic that when a person eliminates all the derogatory, distracting, perhaps even sinful practices from his life and focuses his attention on the Word of God, he is bound to prosper in the totality of his life, including his finances.

The Biblical Visionary

When any person begins to see what God can do in his life, when he, like Isaiah, sees the Lord—in all His holiness, His majesty, His beauty—and desires to be one with Him, then he will begin to see life in its true perspective.

And when that person renews his mind in God's Word (see Rom. 12:2) so that he begins to *think* God's Words, then the vision of what God is will begin to grip him. When that happens to a person, he will never again be able to live complacently in the nether world of no goals, no plans, no projections, and no *visions*.

He will begin to look around him and ask God, "What can I do to better my circumstances? What can I do to better the circumstances of others? How can I best share the good news that has so changed me?" Then that person will begin to plan. Plans and visions changed my life.

As a young man, I had made plans for what I had hoped would be an exciting journalism career. Before I met Jesus Christ as my Savior as a nineteen-year-old college student, I had ambitions to become the sports editor of some major metropolitan newspaper. After becoming a Christian, those dreams and plans were directed toward Christian journalism and religious book publication work. And God granted me the privilege of having much of this dream fulfilled in an association for a number of years with a wonderful Christian book-publishing concern.

Then, in 1948, I shared in the first International Congress on World Evangelism in Switzerland. There, meeting with many men and women whose names later became household words in evangelical circles, God really gripped my heart with the need for world evangelization. It was something I could not escape. I prayed to the Lord for His direction in my part in the Great Commission. From that experience, my career was directed down other paths and my plans were dramatically changed. A new vision gripped my spirit, one which has not left me across the years.

"Where there is no vision, the people perish" (Prov. 29:18 KJV). Where there is no vision, an organization will crumble and moulder in the dust. History is filled with reports of nations that slowed, stumbled, then came to a complete halt in their progress—because the original goals and impetus of their great leaders died with the men themselves.

Similarly, the *Wall Street Journal* and other business publications are replete with reports of business failures. It is true that many of these businesses failed because of poor management and inadequate financing. But it is even more true that hosts of them failed because of *the lack of vision.*

This same principle holds for Christian organizations. Almost weekly I learn of a Christian organization that has folded. Several times a year I learn of another Christian publication that has gone out of business. I frequently get word of outstanding men and women of God who have changed their minds about the validity of the message and have gone back to their fishing. And I am deeply grieved.

Why have they failed? In my experience, most businesses,

most churches, most organizations fail for a single major reason—lack of vision.

For God-anointed and God-commissioned administrators, the challenges that lie ahead are still more fraught with glorious opportunities than the halcyon past or present. And God still provides dreams and visions for those who are willing to seek Him.

Right here is a good place to discuss a matter that's often asked of me: "What do you do when an employee doesn't work out? How do you handle the situation when you must let him go?"

To begin with, my philosophy has always been that if a person whom I have hired to do a task has failed in his execution of the job, it's not always his fault. In fact, I usually accept the responsibility for his failure. The reason for this is twofold: I believe (1) that if I had carefully assessed the position *and* had thoroughly checked out the person in order to match the two, he *would have accomplished* the task he was hired to do; and (2) if I had effectively made the assignment to this person, making it crystal clear what was expected of him and what the job entailed, he would have been able to perform as expected.

So you see, I believe that an experienced, effective administrator bears the responsibility of matching the person with the job. If he does so, that individual will perform and the project will be completed—on time and with excellence.

Of course there are exceptions to this maxim. But my experience has shown me that they are rare. In either case, when an individual has been engaged to do a job, has done his best, and has not been able to cut it, then I do one of two things.

I call the individual in and inform him of the facts I have outlined above, accepting the responsibility for his inability to perform as desired. If, after the above discussion, the employee still wants to stay with us, I will seek to locate a position that fits him, train him if necessary, and give him another opportunity.

However, if for any reason he no longer wishes to stay with us, I will provide him with a generous severance pay and an honest letter of recommendation.

The final choice is up to the employee. When I call him in I lay out the facts as I see them, then give him an opportunity to respond. Depending upon his response, I ask him "Given the right position, is it your desire to remain with us?" If his answer is positive, I give him some options, which he may accept within an agreed upon time.

Of course, if the employee's attitude is resistant or contentious, that's a totally different matter. In that case, I will simply provide him with severance pay and a letter of recommendation. But if he truly desires to work, I allow him the opportunity to do so and to prove himself.

CHAPTER 12

Known by Their Fruit

Good administrators aren't born; they grow. They develop. Even when someone's personal gift from God is administration, that doesn't mean he will become a fully adequate administrator overnight. The same is true of one whose gift is teaching; one would not expect him to be teaching thousands when he is yet a fledgling.

Learning to administer takes time—time and shaping and molding by the Spirit of God.

Jesus revealed this truth to His disciples. In one of His final teaching discourses to the men He had trained to carry on His kingdom work, Jesus said, "The Holy Spirit, whom the Father will send in My name, He will teach you all things" (John 14:26).

Living Expectantly

Unless taken in context, these words could certainly lead to presumption and error. But taken *in context*, Jesus was saying that any of His children, who were committed to His cause, could expect the Holy Spirit to teach them how to effectively serve in His name.

As a young administrator, this was a comforting bit of knowledge for me. There were many times in my early years (and there are frequent times still) when I called urgently upon the Holy Spirit to teach me how to administer. I remember, when I first began serving with Youth for Christ, that we had so many sharp and beautifully committed young men who came into our ministry. They were aggressive, often poorly trained and ill-equipped for ministry—and yet so eager to minister with other young people. I, too, was new and inexperienced in international youth evangelism. Doors were opening across the world faster than we could possibly enter them, and it meant that we really had to lean hard on the Lord for His wisdom and direction.

Many were the all-night prayer meetings we held—and always the Lord would meet us in a very special way. Those prayer meetings were unforgettable occasions for all of us in leadership who shared in them. I learned early on that in tough administrative decisions, God is faithful in giving a special sense of wisdom and His direction. He proved this to us time without number in those early days as I was first getting my feet wet.

More recently, when the suggestion was first made that I become the president of World Vision, I knew that even with a backlog of experience in administration, I would need the Holy Spirit to teach me how to step into this heavy and vitally important new assignment.

I asked close counselors to pray with me about this challenge. I had been making other plans for my work and ministry in World Vision, and taking on added responsibilities was not part of my program! Rather, I felt I wanted a lessened administrative role, to be freer for other kinds of ministry. God, however, had other plans. Those I counseled with felt that there was further opportunity, at least for a short period of time, to extend the gift of administration in a wider range. It has been a constant source of encouragement to me to note how God makes our earlier experiences—both our triumphs and failures—redemptive in such situations.

Jesus told His followers that men of God would be known by their fruit. "Do men gather grapes from thornbushes or figs from thistles? Even so, every good tree bears good fruit" (Matt. 7:16–17).

I determined early in my ministry that I would seek to be one who bore good fruit. I have sought to work toward that goal. And though I have most gratefully received some accolades for performance, the one I am most eagerly looking forward to is, "Well done," from the Master Himself. I have wanted to strive, like the apostle Paul, to forget "those things which are behind and [reach] forward to those things which are ahead," to "press toward the goal for the prize of the upward call of God in Christ Jesus" (Phil. 3:13–14).

Administrative Guidelines

Allow me to share with you a few of the guidelines that I use in my efforts in this regard. Not all of them are original, but I have made them mine. And as I share them with you, I trust that they will help you as they have helped me.

1. *I made the unequivocal decision to put Jesus first in everything.* Although I had been brought up in a Christian home, I did not accept the Lord Jesus Christ into my life until my first year in college. It was there, through the influence of another student, who now for more than four decades has been my wife, that I came to a personal relationship with the Savior. I had been running from Him for many years, but Dorothy's influence on me had a profound effect. She had determined, before she came to college, not to date fellows who were not Christians. Even though we became friends, she refused to go out with me on dates because I was not a believer. The Lord used that testimony in my life, together with many other dramatic influences, and ultimately led me to a place of surrender to Himself. My conversion was a dramatic, unforgettable, and unshakable

experience. It was at that moment of decision I determined that, as best I knew how, I would seek always to put Christ first in my life.

I can honestly say that from that moment in my life, I have sought to hew to the line in my relationship to my Lord. Admittedly, I have failed time without number, and a forgiving God has always met me at my point of need. That decision has been of enormous benefit to me throughout my life. And I can say now, looking back over a good number of years, that that decision which I made between myself and God has made it much easier to make decisions between myself and my fellow man.

2. Early in my walk of faith, *I chose to make daily prayer an unchanging essential.* My times with my Lord are both personal and precious. As a result, the maxim "Prayer changes things" is more than a wall plaque to me. Prayer works! It changes things and organizations. It changes people. It changed and changes me.

When I first went to World Vision, I learned that we were 90 to 120 days behind in some of our accounts payable, delinquent on promised orphan payments, and struggling to stay alive financially. Not once, but several times, our controller would tell me that we didn't have enough money in the bank to meet our payroll.

It was in these times of stress that I would call our staff together for a late night prayer meeting. Often we would meet from early evening until after midnight, seeking the Lord to help us meet our financial needs. And God always was faithful to meet our needs—often the very next day! Spiritual administration begins—and ends—with a full dependence on God to do His work with and in us by His Holy Spirit. It isn't only in times of stress, however, that we need Him in our leadership. We must constantly depend on His guidance and direction.

3. Another maxim I have adopted that has saved hours and

days of valuable kingdom time is that *I have sought never to shirk from facing unpleasant tasks.* I am human, as are we all, and I no more enjoy handling an angry or recalcitrant employee than the next person. But I believe that I have saved much valuable emotional energy and an inestimable amount of God's time by facing up to my responsibilities and handling situations as they arise.

4. Another item I believe will be helpful to administrators, especially younger ones, has to do with finances. *I have kept my personal and business finances totally separate at all times.* I never commingle monies. When I am traveling for World Vision, I don't put my money and the company's money together. Aside from the morality involved, an immense amount of time is saved when I return from travels.

While I am on the subject of finances, I must indicate that temptations regarding money have brought many good men to an untimely termination of an otherwise successful career. I never become involved in any transaction that might even look like I could have a vested interest in it on a financial basis.

The Fruit of Righteousness

Jesus said we would be recognized by our fruit. The writer of Proverbs said, "The fruit of the righteous is a tree of life" (Prov. 11:30). This brings to mind the psalmist's words, that the righteous man "shall be like a tree . . . that brings forth its fruit in its season" (Ps. 1:3).

And what, exactly, is the "fruit" of the righteous? The answer to this question is found in Galatians. There the apostle Paul tells us that the fruit which the Holy Spirit's presence within us accomplishes "is love, joy (gladness), peace, patience (an even temper, forbearance), kindness, goodness (benevolence), faithfulness; (meekness, humility), gentleness, self-control (self-restraint, continence). Against such things there is no law [that can bring a charge]" (Gal. 5:22–23, *Amplified Bible*).

As I understand this inspired Word from God, these nine different elements are not nine different fruits (plural). But, rather, they are simply nine different dimensions or manifestations of the work the Holy Spirit is doing within a person's life.

Hence, as a Christian administrator, I am not to bear one or two of the items listed above. I'm to bear them all. They are to be an integral, inseparable part of my nature. I am to evidence, for example, love—not just sometimes—but all the time.

I am to speak with *love*, to transact personal and corporate relationships in love. I am to evidence the loving spirit of Jesus with my colleagues, with my office staff, with all whom I meet. I am to let my "love be sincere—a real thing; [I am to] hate what is evil (loathe all ungodliness, turn in horror from wickedness), but to hold fast to that which is good. [I am, along with all my Christian brothers, commanded to] Love one another with brotherly affection—as members of one family" (Rom. 12:9–10, *Amplified Bible*).

Joy should be part and parcel of my personality. Not necessarily exuberant, gushy-type joy; but deep, inward joy. I believe that's what Nehemiah was referring to when he said, "for the joy of the LORD is your strength" (Neh. 8:10). There is scarcely anything more depressing to an employee than to be ushered into his administrator's office and to be subjected to a drab, joyless conversation or a time of tedious instruction or even a dull job interview.

The question comes to my mind, that if, indeed, "the joy of the LORD *is* my strength," then what happens to my energy when joy subsides? Do I lose my strength? I believe that does happen. When I allow myself to become embroiled in emotional turmoil, then my joy flees; consequently I have that "drained of energy" feeling. My strength and energy have left me. Consequently, I treasure the "joy of the LORD" and consciously conduct my business in a joyful manner.

What about peace?

Peace is an absolute necessity in my life and in my office. The opposite of peace, to me, is strife, and I will do everything to prevent strife from developing in my office. Jesus said, "Peace I leave with you, My peace I give to you; not as the world gives do I give to you. Let not your heart be troubled, neither let it be afraid." The last part of this verse in John 14:27 reads in the *Amplified Bible*: "Stop allowing yourselves to be agitated and disturbed; and do not permit yourselves to be fearful and intimidated and cowardly and unsettled."

When strife enters a life, a home, or an office, then there is also "confusion and every evil thing" (James 3:16). Since peace is part of my relationship with Jesus, I want always to seek to maintain it in every other relationship.

Patience is something that doesn't come naturally to me. I want to "get on with it," to "get the job done," to "get moving." But I believe that over the years the Holy Spirit has been lovingly tempering me in this area. And I realize that in this area, as with all the fruit of the Spirit, there needs to be a constant awareness of "cultivating" the fruit.

Kindness or, as the King James Version puts it, "gentleness," is an attribute manifested by the Lord Jesus and one He expects to be evidenced by us in all that we do. Jesus' kindness was manifested in His treatment of all peoples, regardless of social or economic factors. He was gentle and kind to children, to the blind, to lepers, to the sick.

So when we, evidencing the fruit of the Spirit, manifest this attribute as He did, we are walking as Jesus walked. A scriptural command I have sought to keep ever in mind is the one written by Paul to the church at Ephesus. "And be kind to one another," he said, "tenderhearted, forgiving one another, just as God in Christ also forgave you" (Eph. 4:32).

Goodness ("benevolence" in the *Amplified Version*) is an intrinsic part of the Spirit-life and the Spirit-walk. The word means uprightness, generosity, and in Hebrew thinking is also a euphemism for God. So for a believer to evidence this characteristic is to be Godlike. Of the brothers and sisters in the church at Rome, Paul said, "I . . . am confident concerning you . . . that you also are full of goodness" (Rom. 15:14).

Faith (in the King James Version), and "faithfulness" in some other versions, infers loyalty—both to the Father and to Jesus—and also to the family of God. As an administrator, I value faithfulness in an employee, ranking it very high on my personal scale of values. To me, faithfulness includes the synonymous virtues of integrity and honesty.

The word *meekness*, the eighth portion of this cluster, is a word that has often been misunderstood. It does not, as we have been taught in many circles, mean a Caspar Milquetoast personality, a willingness to be run over and walked on. Jesus said, "Blessed are the meek" (Matt. 5:5). To the Jews this word meant (and still means) *righteous*. They are the ones who bind themselves to the rule of God.

Understood in this way, I have sought to find and assign these "righteous seekers-after-God" on my staff. There can be no better way to promote a spiritual atmosphere, a place where God's presence is felt and God's business is transacted, than where these men and women congregate. Jesus said of them that they "shall inherit the earth" (Matt. 5:5). I praise the Lord for this because, by God's definition, I am among that group.

The last in this cluster of fruit is *self-control*, or self-restraint. Without this one, all the others would amount to little or nothing. In World Vision I greatly admire and respect the colleagues and employees who evidence this quality. In fact, none of our people without this quality will rise to places of significant leadership.

Known by Our Fruit

I have said all the above to say this: Jesus said we (His people) would be known by the fruit we bear (see Matt. 13:33). If we bear good fruit, perfect fruit, unspotted and unsullied fruit, we enhance all that the kingdom of God is.

If the fruit we bear offends God we will not be among the blessed ones (see Ps. 1:4–6). In fact, Psalm 1:6 assures us that "the way of the ungodly shall perish."

"Known by their fruit"—that's all of us, administrators and nonadministrators alike. To be known by our fruit, we must bear that fruit. And to bear that fruit, we must allow the Spirit of God to flow through us because, in the final analysis, *He is the bearer of the fruit.*

Personal Accountability

This matter of fruit bearing is of the utmost importance. It is so important, in fact, that I'm going to address directly *my personal accountability,* as a man of God—both *to* God and *for* God. I have desired to produce excellent fruit. Conversely, I have sought never to be satisfied with anything less than the best.

This means that as an administrator whom God has placed in a position of leadership, I dare not allow my position to lead me into the trap of thinking that I am above the rules or that I am not responsible to anyone. As president of World Vision, I am ultimately responsible *for* the leadership of more than two thousand employees in over eighty nations.

In addition to being responsible for these people, I am also responsible *to* the World Vision board. I seek never to lose sight of either consideration. But above and beyond both of the others is my responsibility to my Master. That is of the utmost concern to me, because I am determined that I will not "have run my race in vain" (Gal. 2:2 NIV).

Many years ago I heard a friend of mine, Pastor Ray Stedman, talk about a special group of men he had gathered around him to meet with him on a weekly basis. These men were not all members of his congregation, but were close friends who held each accountable in their spiritual walk. He said his experience with those men was one of the most meaningful experiences in his life.

After thinking about it, and realizing the need for such accountability in my own life, I talked to my pastor about it. Dr. Ray Ortlund was interested. He expressed similar deep needs and feelings, so we met a couple of times to discuss the concept. Then we invited several men to meet with us. Some of the original group dropped out, but ultimately there were six of us who met together for more than ten years in a local restaurant. We called it the 2/4/6 Club, indicating that there were six of us, who met on the second and fourth Friday mornings of each month for breakfast. We met at 7:00 A.M. for approximately an hour and a half.

It was not a prayer group; although we did pray together. It was not a Bible study group; although we did look into the Word together. It was a time of meeting and growing together, appreciating each other and sharing our individual spiritual pilgrimages. There was no appointed leader and no agenda for the meetings. We met to share experiences, to laugh, to weep. We rejoiced together in our successes. We also shared and wept together over our failures.

Those meetings proved to be a tremendously significant experience in my life. The constituency of the group has changed now, and I meet with another group on a monthly basis, but not quite in the same depth as the earlier group.

During one of our times together, we decided that each of us needed to develop a strategy for spiritual effectiveness. We agreed that in the month following we would each develop such a strategy and share it with the group. Though that happened a dozen or so years ago, I still carry in my wallet what has become a tattered yellow card. The heading reads: "A Spiritual Strategy for Maximum Spiritual Effectiveness."

This is very personal to me, and I have never before revealed to anyone outside the other five men in the 2/4/6 Club the contents of that card. However, I have reviewed the list frequently and have tried to keep my feet to the fire regarding the following six challenges. Here they are:

1. I deliberately place myself daily before God to allow Him to use me as He wills (Romans 12:1–2).
2. Ask God at a specific time *daily* to reveal His strategy and will for me that day.
3. Set and achieve a goal for personal spiritual development through reading one significant book per week.
4. Isolate a known point of weakness (spiritually), and work on it with the help of the Holy Spirit to correct and improve this weakness.
5. Make a study of several Bible people who are good examples—and seek deliberately to emulate them in their strong points.
6. Set up a measuring device to check spiritual development (quantitatively) and measure regularly.

I am convinced that every mature Christian needs to be identified with three types or groups of people. One—we all need a Barnabas, a "Son of Encouragement" (Acts 4:36). Paul had his Barnabas, who counseled him early in his ministry. Barnabas traveled with Paul, prayed with him, shared with him. And, in context, I am certain that Barnabas gave Paul strong and effective spiritual guidance. All of us need that.

As indicated earlier, I have long had a Barnabas in my life, Dr. Carlton Booth, a retired seminary professor beloved by thousands. He has an office with us now in World Vision where he serves as secretary-treasurer of our board.

Two—I am convinced that every Christian ought to have a Timothy—someone to whom he totally gives of himself. Paul had his Timothy, his "son in the faith" (1 Tim. 1:2). They, too, traveled, shared, wept, and rejoiced together.

Three—I believe that every Christian needs to be a part of an accountability group such as I have just described. Such a group would help him to bear the kind of fruit Jesus discusses in John, chapter 15. We dare not be "lone rangers" in our spiritual pilgrimage. The members of our accountability group will watch us, pray for us, and be aware of our progress. As I mentioned above, each one needs such a group to report to, who will help keep him in check.

Such a group, I am convinced, is not a luxury; it's a necessity. We all need each other. In the Body of Christ none of us can be completely independent of each other. Even though we may act like it on occasion, God will ultimately show us just how much we do need each other.

The apostle Paul spoke very pointedly on this subject:

> As it is, there are many parts, but one body. The eye cannot say to the hand, "I don't need you!" And the head cannot say to the feet, "I don't need you!" On the contrary, those parts of the body that seem to be weaker are indispensable, and the parts that we think are less honorable we treat with special honor. And the parts that are unpresentable are treated with special modesty, while our presentable parts need no special treatment. But God has combined the members of the body and has given greater honor to the parts that lacked it, so that there should be no division in the body, but that its parts should have equal concern for each other. If one part suffers, every part suffers with it; if one part is honored, every part rejoices with it. Now you are the body of Christ, and each one of you is a part of it (1 Cor. 12:20–27, NIV).

I have been deeply impressed that in His Body, we are not just one massive body. We are individuals. And each of us carries out a vital function. This obviously means that we are—*we must be*—accountable to one another. John Donne said it as well as anyone, "No man is an island . . . every man is a piece of the continent."

This Scripture in 1 Corinthians sharply focuses for us the inescapable fact that we must share mutual concerns. We must share and participate in our common interests. We do not stand alone, separately and without identity. We are accountable.

Therefore, we dare not remain aloof, isolated, anonymous, as so many do. We must not respond with indifference when our brother cries out to us or when one of our body (a hand, a foot, an eye) is hurting or has gone astray.

We must seek shelter in the "secret place of the Most High." And there, with other members of the divine Body, we "shall abide under the shadow [protection] of the Almighty" (Ps. 91:1).

Such a Body will know no division. And such a Body will stand against all the wiles, all the darts of the enemy.

As an administrator, my purpose in life is to guide men into the truth, to enable them to be all that God intended for them to be. I am accountable unto God for achieving this purpose, and through His power that works in me, I am being enabled to do it.

Some Delightful Absolutes

If there is anything I have learned during my forty-plus years of service in the administrative function, it is that there are few absolutes in administration. But there are some. Let me list a few:

1. *One who has been placed in the office of administration by God will function with joy.* Of course there are times when any administrator will think that he or she would like to trade places with one of the colleagues for whom he or she is responsible. But if a person is truly walking in line with the Holy Spirit's directions, if he is daily abiding in the Word of God (see John 15:7) and has so conducted himself and set up his office as to produce a "strifeless ambience," then he will truly be able to count his work as all joy.

I am convinced this will be so with anyone who has determined his own personal gift, and has then waited upon the Lord until he has been selected for the office most befitting his gifts.

2. *I believe that one's colleagues, family, and friends will note the joy that comes to the one who is thus properly placed.* This has been true almost without exception in my own life. There have been times (for instance, when I have had a tremendously pressing schedule) that some of those closest to me have noted my

temporary dissatisfaction and commented about it. But for the most part, all of those who are close to me have frequently remarked about how much I have continued to enjoy my work.

My wife has reminded me frequently of how much satisfaction I have found in the three careers God has allowed me to have—in religious book publishing, youth evangelism, and world missions. In each, there has been a role for me to exercise the gift of administration in a personally meaningful way which has been most rewarding. And to realize that those closest to me have identified the satisfaction has been most affirming as well.

3. *Despite the heavy and nearly continuous demands that come to an administrator, if he is serving in that position in response to God's call, he will bear up well, personally and emotionally.* My work at World Vision demands a great deal of travel (I long ago lost track of the millions of miles I've flown), yet I find such fulfillment in my administrative duties that I eagerly look forward to each new day and each new week. The reason: I continuously find new challenges and new rewards in my administrative responsibilities.

The effective administrator serving the Lord should believe and accept the fact that God will give him a sense of fulfillment in the daily carrying out of his responsibilities.

One more fact, which I think is almost a maxim among administrators who have been placed in their office by God, is that *they find so much joy in their professional life that they don't necessarily look forward to retirement.* I know I am speaking for myself and many others like me. The joy of serving where you fit brings its own rewards!

The enthusiasm one brings to his work has, I believe, a measurable effect upon even the physical makeup of the body. The apostle Paul seemed to indicate this in Romans 8:11 when he wrote, "If the Spirit of Him who raised Jesus from the dead dwells in you, He who raised Christ from the dead will also give life to your mortal bodies through His Spirit who dwells in you."

I believe that if one is treating his physical body as it deserves to be treated, as a temple of the Holy Spirit—providing it with proper food and rest—that he will rarely be sick. I am so seldom ill that my doctor remarks about it when I visit him for my annual physical checkup.

I don't think for a moment that I am exceptional or that my physique is above normal wear. But it has been my observation that top Christian administrators whose walk with the Lord is consistent generally function relatively free from the physical ailments that many people accept as normal. Don't you agree that the joys of serving where one belongs has much to do with this?

One final word: Throughout my career, I have sought to expend my spiritual energies toward the pursuit of excellence. I seek to make this true in my personal and business relationships, in my home and family life, in my relationship to my God. Having done so and having reaped the benefits that have thus accrued, I want to say with the words of the apostle Paul, "And now, brethren, I commend you to God and to the word of His grace, which is able to build you up and give you an inheritance among all those who are sanctified" (Acts 20:32). May it be so!

Alexander, John W. *Managing Our Work.* rev. ed. Downers Grove, Ill.: Inter-Varsity, 1975.

Allen, Louis A. *The Management Profession.* New York: McGraw-Hill, 1964.

Anderson, James B.; and Jones, Ezra Earl. *The Management of Ministry.* New York: Harper, 1978.

Blanchard, Kenneth. *The One Minute Manager.* San Diego, Cal., Blanchard & Johnson, 1981.

Dayton, Ed; and Engstrom, Ted. *The Art of Management for Christian Leaders.* Waco, Tex.: Word, 1976.

Dayton, Ed; and Engstrom, Ted. *Strategy for Leadership.* Old Tappan, N.J.: Revell, 1979.

Dayton, Ed; and Engstrom, Ted. *Strategy for Living.* Glendale, Cal.: Regal, 1976.

Drucker, Peter F. *The Effective Executive.* New York: Harper, 1967.

Drucker, Peter F. *Managing in Turbulent Times.* New York: Harper, 1980.

Engstrom, Ted W. *The Making of a Christian Leader.* Grand Rapids: Zondervan, 1976.

Gangel, Kenneth. *Competent to Lead.* Chicago: Moody, 1974.

Laird, Donald A. *The Technique of Getting Things Done.* New York: McGraw-Hill, 1947.

Mackenzie, Alec. *The Time Trap: Managing Your Way Out.* New York: American Management Association, 1972.

Naisbitt, John. *Megatrends: Ten New Directions Transforming Our Lives.* New York: Warner Books, 1982.

Peters, Thomas J.; and Waterman, Robert H., Jr. *In Search of Excellence*. New York: Harper, 1982.

Schaller, Lyle E. *Effective Church Planning*. Nashville: Abingdon, 1979.